The Second Coming of Jesus

Pray for
Marilyn Pardes

Eileen Carol
~~E Ilene~~
841 Shady Oak Dr.
95404

539-5771

The Second Coming of Jesus

Meditation and Commentary on the Book of Revelation

Alfred McBride, O. Praem.

Our Sunday Visitor Publishing Division
Our Sunday Visitor, Inc.
Huntington, Indiana 46750

Nihil Obstat: Reverend Joseph A. Fitzmyer, S.J.
                  Censor Deputatus

Imprimatur: Reverend Msgr. William J. Kane
                  Vicar General for the Archdiocese of Washington
                  August 14, 1992

The nihil obstat and imprimatur are official declarations that a book
or pamphlet is free of doctrinal or moral error. No implication is
contained therein that those who have granted the nihil obstat and the
imprimatur agree with the content, opinions or statements expressed.

ISBN: 0-87973-526-0
LCCCN: 92-61979
PRINTED IN THE UNITED STATES OF AMERICA
Cover design by Rebecca J. Heaston

I wish to dedicate this book to some very dear friends: To Dr. William May, editor of my first four books, and to his wife, Dr. Patricia May. I also wish to acknowledge the Divine Word Fathers of Washington, D.C., who have provided me with a spiritual home and hospitality for the years I have been on loan from my Order in this city. In particular, I am grateful to Father John Farley, S.V.D., Brother Robert Zalikowski, S.V.D., Father Ray Sanders, S.V.D., and Dorothy Madey in their business office. Last, I want to remember the kindnesses of Monsignor Robert Lynch, Secretary General of the Bishops' Conference, Sister Elaine McCarron, S.C.N., and Reverend Paul Etienne.

Contents

Introduction.. 9

1 Faith Under Fire 14

2 Gifts of the White Stone and the Morning Star 23

3 Cultural Christians Vs. Faith Christians 33

4 Heaven Opens 42

5 The Lamb Appears.. 48

6 The Four Horsemen Are Coming 53

7 Joyful, Joyful, We Adore Thee....................................... 62

8 Hell Is in Session 71

9 A Closer Look 76

10 Get Ready for Joy 82

11 The Spiritual Power of Christian Witness 87

12 A Woman's Pain — A Dragon's Defeat 93

13 Who Is the Beast? The Antichrist................................104

14 The Mystery Reveals and Conceals 113

15 A Sea of Glass Touched With Fire...............................121

16 The Bowls of God's Wrath...125

17 Who Is the Scarlet Woman? 131

18 The Twilight of the Gods...140

19 The Wedding Feast of the Lamb 148

20 Millennium — Christ's Thousand-Year Reign 156

21 The New Jerusalem — My Happy Home 164

22 Come, Lord Jesus! Yes, I Am Coming Soon!..............173

Introduction

Are You Afraid of the Third Millennium?

What would happen if a pope had a vision that the end of the world was about to happen?

Novelist Morris West asked himself that question and decided it would make a fascinating tale. In his book, *The Clowns of God*, the fictional Pope Gregory XVII has a vision. God calls him to proclaim the "Last Days" and call the world to prepare for the Second Coming of Jesus near the year 2000. He writes an encyclical about it, *In These Last Fateful Years of the Millennium.*

Before it could become public, the college of cardinals convened and decided this was too traumatic for the world. They advised him to resign. If he refused they would declare him insane and force him to abdicate. After reflection, prayer, and consultation, he abdicates and retires to a monastery. The story continues to unfold against a background of superpower rivalry and nuclear threats. For those who want to read the story, I will not spoil matters by revealing the ending.

In Catholic teaching, private visions, whether those received by laity at Lourdes or Fatima, or those that might be given to a pope in the Vatican only require "human faith" from us; we may believe it if we wish. We are only bound to believe the public revelation in the Bible and its interpretation in the tradition and magisterium of the church. Were a pope to have such a vision, his teaching about it would not be part of his infallible or authentic teaching office. Naturally, his important role as chief shepherd of the church would lend compelling credibility to his words, but we still would not be bound to believe what he learned from a private vision.

As the year 2000 approaches, prophecies about the end of the world will increase. We are already familiar with such predictions from fundamentalist Christians and can expect to hear them from mainline Christians as the third millennium approaches. The Book of

Revelation (or Apocalypse) is the favorite resource for these predictors. They back it up with prophetic quotes from the books of Daniel and Ezekiel and the Last Judgment sermons of Jesus, along with the so-called "rapture" scene in I Thessalonians 4:16-17.

The forthcoming surge of millenarian fever has prompted me to examine the Book of Revelation, to see what questions it raises and to note what answers it really gives. Here are some questions I will raise in this meditation and commentary on Revelation.

- Does the Book of Revelation disclose the date of the end of the world?
- Will there be a millennium — a thousand years — of Christian victory on earth?
- Does Scripture justify a belief in a literal "Rapture" that would usher in the millennium?
- Is the "New World Order" after the fall of Communism in Eastern Europe a sign of the beginning of the last days?
- When will the "Seven Years of Tribulation" happen? Or, has it already begun?
- Can we already identify in our own day the incarnation of "The Beast of the Apocalypse"?
- Is there a connection between "666" and satanic cults?
- How are we to decode, with our Christian faith, the riotous range of symbols in Revelation?
- For whom did John write Revelation? The first Christians? Us? Or only those who would live when the Second Coming actually happens?
- Are we living in the last days of the "late, great planet earth?"

These are some of the numerous questions raised by Revelation itself as well as by millenarian Christians. Rather than offering clues to the answers in this introduction, I urge readers to delve into the biblical text of Revelation and to use this book as a guide for interpretation.

Tradition says that John the Apostle and beloved disciple is the author of this book. Ancient church fathers and modern scholars dispute this. The author of the book calls himself John, but gives no further identification. During a Roman persecution of Christians, John the author is arrested and exiled to a penal colony on the island of Patmos, not far from Ephesus and the other six churches mentioned in the book. It is on that spare, mountainous island surrounded by the crystal-like Aegean sea, that John received his visions and recorded them in the Book of Revelation.

To understand his book, we will be helped by remembering these three points about the approach of the author.

1. John uses the apocalyptic form of writing. Apocalypse means revelation. Because apocalyptic writers dwell so much on the catastrophes, disasters, wars, epidemics, and tragedies that accompany both the end of "a" world as well as the end of "the" world, apocalypse connotes revelation as applied to the collapse of the cosmos. Because apocalypse deals with extraordinary times, it uses exceptional language. Stars fall, blood covers the moon, the earth trembles, waters overflow their boundaries, killers roam the earth, mothers weep for their children, empires fall, havoc rules the world.

The Old Testament books of Ezekiel and Daniel use apocalyptic language. They talk about the end of history and the beginning of the messianic age. So also does Jesus in his Last Judgment sermons. More than anyone else in Scripture, John revels in the apocalyptic style. We shall see why he uses it and then realize why it is such an effective way to talk about the truth of God in human affairs.

2. John communicates like a prophet. In Scripture, prophets have three tasks. (a) To call people to repentance and conversion. (b) To explain the meaning of human events — the "signs of the times" — from the viewpoint of God's plan for salvation and his will for us. (c) To predict future actions of God, not with dates and timeliness, but consistent with God's promises and fidelity to his purposes.

John treats the Old Testament like a prophetic treasure trove. Though he never actually quotes it, he borrows freely and lavishly from its teachings. Of his 404 verses in Revelation, 278 of them allude to an Old Testament idea. Always he acts in the prophetic tradition. He calls his readers to moral and spiritual renewal. He unravels the meaning of this world's sufferings and persecutions of believers in the light of the divine plan of redemption. He foretells the fulfillment of God's promises.

3. John offers us a Christ-centered vision to sustain us no matter

how bad things get. Saint Thomas More wrote that "The times are never so bad that a good man cannot live in them." No culture is ever so dreadful that it makes it impossible to be good. Philosopher Peter Kreeft writes that "Bad times are no excuse for bad choices and bad lives." Rough periods of history are "soul making" experiences. It is in the moral challenges of such times that great saints are made. We will see how effectively John makes a case for this principle. He portrays the incontrovertible truth that Jesus is alive. He summons all believers to reaffirm their faith in the Lamb that was slain and is now victorious. In many ways, Revelation is the perfect last word and interpretation of what the gospels are all about.

Pope John Paul II's Third Millennium

I began this introduction with a story about a fictional pope who has an alarming vision about the year 2000. Let me conclude with what a real pope is saying about the new millennium which is about to begin. Throughout his pontificate, Pope John Paul II has said a great deal about the year 2000 and what it means for us. He approaches the issue with a faith-informed optimism. He is never a prophet of gloom and doom. Firmly set in the middle of any message he gives us is Jesus Christ our Savior and the center of the universe and history. We know very well that John Paul is fully aware of the problems in the world and the church, and he discusses such matters often. His faith optimism is set in a context of this sea of troubles.

This is a man seasoned by the persecutions inflicted on him and his country by the two great evil ideologies of our time — Nazism and Communism. Yet no one speaks more of Christian hope than he does. He is excited by the Third Millennium. "It (2000) will be a year of great jubilee. We are in a season of a new Advent. We are already approaching that date, which will recall and reawaken in us our awareness of a key truth of faith. 'The Word became flesh and dwelt among us (Jn. 1:14)' " (*Redemptor Hominis*, 1).

Holding before our attention the magnificent love of God, he teaches that our attachment to Jesus will make a new age possible. The Third Millennium should stimulate us now to a revival of prayer. "Only prayer can prevent all these tasks and difficulties from becoming a source of crisis and make them instead the foundation for more mature achievements during the march of God's People towards the Promised Land in this stage of human history approaching the end of the second millennium" (*Ibid.*, 22).

Of the three themes of Vatican II — Mystery, Communion, Mission — Pope John Paul is never more eloquent than when he deals with Mission. He always connects Mission with evangelizing. This dynamic vision pictures the church in motion, sent by Jesus to the whole planet to share the best news possible for every human being: God's love is the source of human dignity. God's mercy is the real answer to human alienation and sin. God's gift of real life in Jesus is the true divine reply to the hunger for human fulfillment.

We all know that Pope John Paul does more than talk about Mission. Year after year he journeys to the whole world to bring this joyful message of Jesus. Small wonder he rejects the pessimism of the world. Close as he is to the central fire of hope, what else could he preach? Listen to him come to a soaring climax in his encyclical on evangelizing in *The Mission of the Redeemer.*

As the Third Millennium of the redemption draws near, God is preparing a great springtime for Christianity. We can already see its first signs. Both in the non-Christian world and in the traditionally Christian one, people are gradually drawing closer to Gospel values and ideals, a development the church encourages. There is a new consensus about these values: the rejection of violence and war; respect for the human person and for human rights; the desire for freedom, justice and brotherhood, the surmounting of different forms of racism and nationalism; the affirmation of the dignity and role of women. CHRISTIAN HOPE SUSTAINS US (86).

This is how the Chief Shepherd of our church sees the Third Millennium.

I think you will be in for a big surprise when you see how John's Book of Revelation deals with millenniums.

Begin today with his book and this meditative commentary as your guide.

1 Faith Under Fire

On Christmas Day 1991, the Communist flag came down from the Kremlin tower. Seventy years of relentless persecution of Christians ended. In April of that year I stood in St. Yuri's Cathedral in Lvov, Ukraine and heard fellow Catholics sing praises to Christ with unrestrained joy. After decades of oppression, they were free to practice their faith openly. Jesus had cared about them. Their faith was not in vain.

John wrote his Book of Revelation to a Christianity that was barely seventy years old when it faced the beginning of several centuries of persecution. Nero had just paraded through the Roman Forum. Torches, coated with tar and resin lighted his path. The "torches" were the bodies of Christians.

During a summer festival in the Rhone valley in France, the government sponsored a riot against Christians falsely accused of incest and cannibalism. A mob beat and tortured dozens of Christians. They applied hot plates to the body of Sanctus of Vienne until he was one vast bruise. They beheaded others. They forced many to run through a gauntlet of whips to the local arena where they were mauled by wild animals in full view of a frenzied crowd.

The Roman state deprived openly practicing Christians of education, jobs, and property. The systematic hostility of the greatest power on earth frightened and disheartened many early Christians. If they witnessed their faith, their children and families were endangered. Did God care about them? Did Jesus know what was happening? Why didn't Jesus do something about it? Did Jesus care?

John's answer was "yes."

That is what the Book of Revelation is all about.

Jesus was concerned about the pain and confusion of those first Christians, just as in our own time Jesus cared about the millions of

Christians who suffered in Eastern Europe — and still do so in China. There has always been a persecuted church in one form or another. In our day, we know about the political persecution of Christians in the East. We are also aware of the cultural opposition to Christian Catholic teaching in the West.

We seem outmaneuvered and helpless and think that God does not care. Read the Book of Revelation and hear his divine word: "I care." John makes this abundantly clear in chapter one.

The Reason for This Book (1:1-8)

An angel brought John a revelation from Jesus Christ, a message of reassurance and divine concern for the threatened Christian communities. John instructed the leaders of the various communities to read this message out loud at their liturgical gatherings. He blessed those who would read the revelations and those who would hear them with faith and resolve to persevere because of them.

John emphasized that the "time" of their fulfillment was "near."

He was dealing with the outcome of history ("time") at two levels — their own current history in the early church and the end of history itself, which would be ushered in by the Second Coming of Jesus. When he used the expression "near," he never gave a date. The listeners would not know when persecution would end. In fact, not until Constantine freed Christianity in 313, would the first major trial of the church conclude.

Nonetheless, their trust in the ultimate victory of Jesus — whether it happened in their lifetime or not — would sustain and strengthen their faith in the face of formidable opposition. Once they believed Jesus really cared about them in their suffering, they lost their fears. Instead of collapsing in self pity, they shone strong in faith. The blood of the martyrs became the seed of the church.

The colorful and splendid images we will read in this book did not confuse the first readers. This was a "code of glory," a fountain of courage from which they drank because they knew it was the poetry of Jesus telling them he was already so near they could feel him in their bones. They hoped in history's vindication. They already felt it in their hearts.

Humanly speaking, the emperors of Rome had intimidated them. But this revelation awoke in them the experience of the real commander of the universe, Jesus "the ruler of the kings of the earth" (verse 5). The emperor dominated them with a love of power. Jesus freed them from sin by the power of love. He formed them into a spiritual kingdom of justice, mercy and love. As a priestly people, they would affirm the power of the sacred against the encroachment of the secular.

Instead of seeing themselves as a beleaguered minority, they envisioned themselves as witnesses to Christ's kingdom which will prevail over all opposition. Thus the revelation infused them with a positive vision of their role in history despite all appearances. They replaced their cry of abandonment with a hymn of confidence, "To him be glory and power forever!" (verse 6).

They had begun to experience Christ's strength in their inner lives. They trusted he would liberate them from the menace of the state at some point in history. Finally, they interpreted earthly liberation as a dress rehearsal for the final triumph of Jesus in his Second Coming. "Behold, he is coming amid the clouds, and every eye will see him, even those who pierced him" (verse 7). In his glory he will bear the marks of the passion at Calvary, which are at the same time the wounds of his Mystical Body suffering persecution for their witness to love and salvation.

Jesus gathers up all of history in himself, as the Alpha (Beginning) and the Omega (Ending). Alpha and Omega are the first and last letters of the Greek alphabet. This image stretches our perception of time so we see it as God views it. We know that when we are happy, time goes fast. If our plane is late, time seems to drag painfully slow as we keep looking at the clock and the second hand.

Jesus lives in a world of perfect joy where time is neither fast nor slow. There is no time in our sense of the word, just the presence of love and perfect satisfaction. That is why Jesus can be experienced as immediately gathering up all of history from the misty dawn of beginning to the unknowable date of the end. This experience communicates patience and wisdom to us in the midst of pain. We feel caught up in a vision of history that collapses the centuries. Beginning and End are Now in our meditation on Jesus who makes it all happen for us.

The Word of God who began creation with love will end it with love. Those of us who remain faithful know this love already and will experience its benefits now and forever. Those who do not believe will be unable to appreciate the loving beginning of creation, the act of redemptive love in history and fail to respond to it at the end.

From the depth of his prayer on the island of Patmos, John saw all this in a glance and a flash. Time did more than fly by or stand still. Like a rose at dawn, time unfolded into the ecstasy of loving and eternal presence between himself and Jesus Christ. He had felt this absolute love at the Last Supper when his head rested against the heart of Jesus. On Patmos he felt it again. He made heaven present in the Book of Revelation. It may tell us a lot about history. It tells us much more about heaven.

The Vision of Jesus in Glory (1:9-20)

Most scriptural visions describe divine calls to undertake a mission. From the burning bush God called Moses to save Israel from political slavery. From the glory of the temple, God called Isaiah to announce the coming of the Messiah who would save the world from its slavery to sin. From the glory of the Damascus road, God called Paul to be a missionary to the world.

John's vision took place on the island of Patmos. It is near the western coast of present day Turkey. The Roman government used it as a penal colony. John had been arrested for his Christian witness and imprisoned on Patmos. That is why he speaks of his suffering and the endurance he finds in Jesus.

To see Patmos today from a cruise ship is to see its white crags in the midst of the glistening Aegean sea. It offered John some of the imagery that appeared in his writing. He recorded the emerald rainbow after a storm, the door that opened to heaven in the parting of the clouds, the sea so calm that it was like glass and crystal. He longed for a time when the "sea was no more" (21:1) so he could go forth and share Jesus with others. The Orthodox monastery of St. John occupies the southern half of Patmos today.

In the glory of this inaugural vision on Patmos, Jesus called John to bring a message of consolation and hope to the suffering church. In his gospel, John summoned his listeners to faith in the resurrection of Jesus. In the Book of Revelation, John invited the community of faith to have hope in the midst of sorrow.

Jesus as Judge

John beheld Jesus as a man through whom shone his divinity and who comes to judge the world. Jesus wore a long robe and a gold sash, reminiscent of the high priest's robes of the Old Testament. Priests often functioned as judges, as Jesus will here. His hair was white as wool to symbolize Christ's wisdom. We speak of the gray beard of wisdom. Scripture tells of the white hair of wisdom. Jesus is a wise judge.

His eyes glowed with fire because, as supreme judge, no person, place, or thing would escape his penetrating glance. His voice had the timber of a rushing river, the forcefulness of a judge. Human leaders have feet of clay, but Jesus has feet of polished brass. Jesus, the just judge, has the durability of irreproachable character.

He held seven stars in his right hand just as the emperor did, but to show he is the judge of all emperors and princes. A two-edged sword came from his mouth. This popular biblical image of the sword means that God's word cannot be treated indifferently. There will be one of two results. One must either accept it or reject it and take the consequences. In Matthew 25, Jesus describes himself as a judge who will come to separate the sheep from the goats. Those who have fed the hungry and clothed the naked will enter the kingdom. Those who failed to do this will not.

This vivid picture of Jesus belongs to the tradition of apocalyptic imagery in Scripture. Read Daniel 7:13 and following for a similar picture of the Son of Man coming on clouds to judge the world. Compare also the face of Jesus here shining "like the sun at its brightest" to the scene of his Transfiguration in Matthew 17:2. The Jesus of this book is the Christ of glory.

Confronted by such an awesome revelation, John fell at the feet of Jesus as though he had died on the spot. Heavenly manifestations frighten humans, but heaven does not want to scare us. Jesus says to

John, "Do not be afraid" (verse 17b). The mighty of the world enjoy putting people down and intimidating them. The almighty in heaven wants to raise people up, honor human dignity, and take away self-destructive fear.

Write to the Seven Churches

Jesus called John to write letters to the seven churches of Asia. He lists Ephesus, Smyrna, Pergamum, Thyatira, Sardis, Philadelphia, and Laodicea. Many other prominent churches existed besides these. Probably John named these seven because they were connected by the same road and easily reached. In addition, since he had lived at Ephesus, he was most likely familiar with these churches and their membership.

Possibly, he often preached to them and celebrated the Breaking of the Bread in their midst. He knew them personally and loved them. He was their special pastor, the sole surviving apostle from the original twelve. From them his message could then go forth to the whole church. That must be why he calls them his seven stars and seven lampstands (verse 20). As stars they can be angelic messengers to the full church. As lampstands they can be lights of faith to all believers.

Jesus Walks With Us in Our Pain

We have noted that John borrowed visual details about the Son of Man from the Book of Daniel. He also adopted a teaching from Daniel, chapter 3, that God walks with us in our suffering. During the captivity of the Jews in Babylon, the king had a statue of himself erected and ordered all people to worship it. Three young Jewish men rebelled against this affront to their faith in the living God.

The king ordered them to be thrown into a fiery furnace. An odd thing happened. The young men walked through the fire unharmed. The fire had no power over their bodies. It did not singe their hair or consume their clothes. They began singing loudly the praises of God. Hearing the music, the guards checked on them and saw this amazing event. More astonishing was the sight of a fourth man walking with them. They reported this to the king, saying, "the fourth looks like a son of God" (verse 92). The fourth person was God walking with the young men in the midst of their persecution.

Isaiah wrote of God's compassion for those in pain with words that echo this story from Daniel. "When you pass through the . . . rivers you shall not drown. When you walk through fire, you shall not be burned; the flames shall not consume you" (Is. 43:2). God wants to walk with us in our suffering. He did this visibly in his Son, Jesus Christ. Though he will not remove all pain from this life, he will be in our souls to give us hope and meaning despite our suffering. Pain and death are the result of sin.

Jesus never sinned, but endured sin's effects — physical, emotional, and spiritual pain. He did this for three reasons. (1) To identify with our pain. He, Son of God, knows what it is like. That is the very realistic source of his compassion. (2) To make voluntary acceptance of suffering and death a means to redeem us from sin, the cause of suffering and death. (3) To invite us to unite our pain and death with his for the forgiveness of sins and liberation from sin's power over us.

This first chapter of the Book of Revelation makes the same message abundantly clear. John is suffering in the Patmos prison. All believers everywhere belong to a persecuted minority. Worried, nervous, and threatened, they fear that God has forgotten them. They fret that he does not care what happens to them.

Into this crisis situation comes Jesus Christ, clothed in the power symbols of divinity and judgment. Until that moment God's people felt lost and at the mercy of the forces of history. Now arrives Jesus who is in command of history. He is not above and beyond them. He is not far away in the unattainable reaches of the heavens. He is not indifferent to their pain. He becomes intimate with them. He walks among the seven lampstands of the seven churches. He enters into the deepest wells of awareness of the apostle John. Through him he touches the consciousness of every believer. They may be in a fiery furnace of hostility of the evil empire, but Jesus walks with them in their pain.

He will not immediately take away their suffering. Nor will he tell them when the storms of suffering will pass. But by his powerful and intimate presence, he instills them with the courage that purifies their faith. With a voice, as loud as a trumpet, he gives them hope that eventually his judgment will cause the end of the persecution that afflicts them. With the force of a rushing river, he confirms the truth that all evil and sinful powers will lose out in the end when he comes visibly "on the clouds of heaven," at his Second Coming.

If the Book of Revelation is a symphony, this first chapter is the overture. All the themes are here. Every chapter after this spells out in detail what is set out in this first one. In its broadest terms, Revelation is a theology of suffering, a gift from God to help those first Christians — and us today — a method for making sense out of our pain.

The Gospel narratives of the passion spell out how Jesus did this in his earthly life. Revelation tells us how the Jesus of glory accomplishes the impact of his passion in our human history.

Today we may not fully appreciate the menace felt by the Christians of the first century. We may not even have fully grasped the agony of our fellow Christians under Communism. But we all know our personal and family sufferings and we are aware of the disdain of our secular culture toward our Christian commitment and teachings. Revelation is just as much a response to our situation as it has been to all other suffering Christians everywhere and in all times. Does God care for us? You bet he does.

Reflection

1. How do films, TV, popular music, novels, and opinion makers in our magazines and newspapers teach messages contrary to the Gospel?
2. What are the forms of pain in my life and that of my family?
3. Where are Christians suffering political persecution for their faith in our world today?
4. What is the response of Jesus to my pain?
5. Why did Jesus suffer pain and death?
6. What evidence do I have that Jesus cares about me?
7. Why does Jesus refrain from giving exact dates about the end of

my pain, the persecution of Christians, or the end of the world?

8. What are the signs of Christian hope in my life?
9. What saints of history or people in today's church give me lots of hope?
10. What lessons have I learned from this first chapter?

Prayer

Jesus, Lord of history and Christ of glory, I praise you for your presence to us in our pain. I thank you for walking with us in our suffering. I am grateful that you have given me a way to make sense out of suffering. You are the rock of my life in a fast-moving world. You are pure love in a world of selfishness. Enliven my faith. Increase my hope. Fill me with the love that never stops.

2 Gifts of the White Stone and the Morning Star

Think of House Churches

Chapters 2 and 3 record John's letters to seven churches. Remember this is the first century of Christianity. The term *churches* refers to the Christian communities in the seven cities. There were no church buildings as we now know them. Christians gathered in designated homes or "house churches." Ordained bishops and presbyters (priests) presided at the liturgies. Paul speaks of this when he writes, "Greet also the church at their house" (Rom. 16:5).

There were no cathedrals, no basilicas, no bell towers, no spires with crosses on top of them, no visible evidence to the public eye of a worship dwelling. In fact the anonymity of the worship space protected the believers from notice by the watchful eye of the government. I myself attended an "underground" liturgy in a house church in Czechoslovakia in 1990 before the freedom granted to religion. Church buildings, as we are familiar with them, did not come into existence until the liberation of the church under Constantine in A.D. 313.

Each of the seven cities mentioned here would have several house churches. Believers gathered to celebrate Eucharist in the setting of a meal, recalling the setting of the Last Supper and of Pass-over meals. The context of a meal in a domestic space makes us think of hospitality, an intimate gathering of friends, a feeling of comradeship.

Such house liturgies were not without their problems as Paul noted in Corinth. "I hear that when you meet as a church, there are divisions among you. . . . When you meet in one place, then, it is not to eat the Lord's Supper, for in eating, each one goes ahead with his own supper, and one goes hungry while another gets drunk. Do you now have houses in which you can eat and drink? Or do you show contempt for the church of God?" (I Cor. 11:18-22).

The description implies that people brought their own food and drink for the meal that accompanied Eucharist, something like brown-bagging a meal. Paul told them that it was scandalous for them not to share their abundance with the poorer members, and shameful for them to get drunk just after celebrating Eucharist.

Paul repeated Christ's words of the institution of the Eucharist and concluded by pointing out that Eucharist is a making present of the sacrificial and saving death of Jesus. "For as often as you eat this bread and drink the cup, you proclaim the death of the Lord until he comes" (I Cor. 11:26). In other words, Eucharist was held in people's homes. Its meaning should result in charitable and temperate behavior. More importantly, it united the participants to the saving power of the death of Jesus.

These comments on house churches will orient you to what John would have visualized in writing to them. On the one hand, he would be speaking to the church as a spiritual community of faith, the Body of Christ. On the other hand, the physical setting was that of a cluster of house churches in the seven cities. This is where they celebrated Eucharist, heard the Word of God, and discussed their faith and church business.

Each of the seven letters contains these common elements:
1. Jesus commands John to write the letter.
2. Different aspects of Christ's glory are described.
3. Jesus always says, "I know" your situation.
4. Jesus proceeds to affirm the positive virtues of a given church and criticize its negative behavior.
5. Jesus concludes with an exhortation that either calls for a change in behavior or perseverance in fidelity.

The most interesting feature of these letters is their message that the real threat to the churches is not external persecution but internal moral, spiritual, and faith problems. With this background we now look at each letter.

Ephesus — The Loss of "First Love" (2:1-7)

Of the seven cities, Ephesus was the largest and probably had the most Christians. Paul had spent two years there evangelizing the community and later wrote a major epistle to the Ephesians. Tradition tells us that John the apostle lived there with the Blessed Mother, whom he took care of until her death. Pilgrims today can visit the "House of Mary" on a plateau overlooking the city.

Ephesus boasted a population of 250,000 people, extensive marble buildings, and the Temple of Diana, considered to be one of the seven wonders of the world. Currently being restored, Ephesus today is one of the best preserved of the cities of classical times.

The seven letters all begin with an address to the angel of the particular church. The angel is the bishop or pastor of the local congregations. John expects the angel to communicate the message of Jesus to his people.

Jesus speaks to them as a divine leader, holding a symbol of power in his hands — the royal scepter with seven stars emanating from it. He brings them spiritual power to cope with their problems. At the same time, he reminds them he is no faraway God. He declares his intimacy with them, for he "walks in the midst of the seven gold lampstands" (verse 1). Jesus is as close to them as the heartaches they suffer.

Jesus knows them personally. He praises their endurance in trials and commends them for rejecting the false teachings of itinerant preachers, who passed themselves off as apostles. Paul predicted this would happen and said as much to his friends at Miletus. "I know that after my departure savage wolves will come among you, and they will not spare the flock" (Acts 20:29).

In our day we have some traveling lecturers and columnists who claim to be teaching the real message of Jesus, but in fact are not. They divide the church, promote hostility between the leadership and the people, and corrode the unity of the faith.

Having complimented them on their astute rejection of harmful teachers, Jesus confronted them with their fatal spiritual flaw. "I hold this against you: you have lost the love you had at first" (verse 4). The atmosphere of fear, brought on by the persecution, damaged the practice of Christian love which they should have for themselves, others, and God. Fear poisons love.

That is why John urged people to get rid of fear, for "There is no fear in love, but perfect love drives out fear" (I Jn. 4:18). Jesus wants to arouse the original dream of love to which they committed themselves at their baptism. The best response to their external problems is a renewal of their inner lives. Let go of fear. Welcome love back to your hearts. They must repent, convert, return to the vision of love, else they will cease to be a lampstand, a light of true Christianity, a genuine witness against the power of external darkness.

Sacrilegious Food

The text at this point mentions the Ephesian repudiation of the Nicolaitans. Presently, we do not know who these people were. Verse 14 of this chapter connects them with advocating lust and eating meat sacrificed to idols. We do know that local butcher shops often sold such meat which had an idolatrous seal of approval. Devout members of idol religions would buy it. Often Christians purchased it as well, possibly because it was of better quality or cheaper. The church opposed this because it made it seem that the Christian diners were sharing in a pagan religion. Even today our orthodox Jewish friends will only eat kosher, or approved, meat.

The Tree of Immortality

Jesus tells them that if they return to love they will eat of better food from the "tree of life that is in the garden of God" (verse 7). The allusion is to the Genesis story. In the Garden of Eden God had planted various trees that were delightful to look at and good for food. Among these were the Tree of Life and the Tree of the Knowledge of Good and Evil (Gen. 2:9). God forbade Adam and Eve to eat of the Tree of the Knowledge of Good and Evil. As we all know, the serpent successfully tempted them to eat the fruit of this tree. Genesis says they were then banished from Eden. Regarding the

Tree of Life, they were forbidden to eat from it and thus be able to live forever (cf. Gen. 3:22). In other words, had they obeyed God they would not have died.

The Tree of Life was a well known sacred symbol in ancient civilizations and was often portrayed in their art works. It was a way of answering the question, "Why do people die?" The answer was that they did something wrong and so were deprived of the food of the gods, the food of immortality. The Greeks called such food, "ambrosia." Assyrian artists depicted the sacred tree on their wall carvings. On the isle of Crete one can still see a sculpture of such a tree with goats eating from it. The fathers of the church considered the cross to be the real Tree of Life, the source of our eternal life.

Jesus promised the Christians of Ephesus that their fidelity would assure them the reward of eternal life. They would eat of the Tree of Life. Already, at their Eucharists, they were partaking of the Bread of Life. The sooner they learned to let go of their fears and anxieties and permit the divine love which they received in the breaking of the bread to possess their hearts, the quicker would they begin to live, even here on earth, the life of love that characterizes eternal life.

Smyrna: A Poor Church in a Rich City (2:8-11)

Jesus portrays himself as the Risen Christ to the church of Smyrna. The author of the original creation presents himself as the new creation to which they should aspire. By their baptism they had put on this new life. In Jesus they could see how this new life looks in its final form.

Smyrna, today called Izmir by the Turks, was a port city on the west coast of Asia Minor. Its well-protected harbor made it an ideal location for maritime trade. Two centuries before Christ, Smyrna foresaw the rising star of Rome. Its leaders established political and economic ties with the Romans. This protected the city from a military threat posed by Syria to the east and from a naval blockade by the island nation of Rhodes to the west.

To strengthen its bond to Rome, Smyrna secured permission to build the world's second temple to the emperor Tiberius, thus sealing the link to Rome by the spiritual ties of emperor worship. It was proud of its Caesar cult. People admired this city for the majesty of its public buildings. A crown of white pillared structures ringed the summit of Mount Pagos that was the backdrop of Smyrna. Here was a wealthy city, having many things of which to be proud.

The only people who did not share in Smyrna's abundance were the Christians. Some were poor because they belonged to the working class who did the menial tasks for the rich. Jesus had told his disciples that the kingdom of God would be Good News for the poor. In fact they turned out to be among the first and most enthusiastic converts to Christianity. Other Christians in Smyrna became poor because they joined a religion outlawed by the empire. Shunned by their former business contacts, they struggled to make a living.

Jesus speaks sympathetically to his poverty stricken flock. "I know your tribulation and poverty" (verse 9). He commends them for being rich in faith and obedience to the demands of the Gospel.

He also recognizes they have suffered from being slandered by the local Jewish leaders, whom he calls the "Synagogue of Satan." No details are given. Jesus himself had been falsely accused by the Sanhedrin. Now the Body of Christ at Smyrna carries a similar cross in its own passion.

Jesus does not deceive them with easy promises of a quick deliverance. Prison and more suffering lay ahead for them. Their faith would be tested more in the days ahead. Their ordeal will last for "ten days." This little number contrasts the brevity of their earthly pain with the endless, eternal joy that will come to those who persevere.

Jesus urges them to remain faithful, even if this means violent death and martyrdom. As they gaze on the magnificent crown of buildings on Mount Pagos, they hear Christ's words of absolute assurance, "I will give you the crown of life" (verse 10). They need not fear the "second death," which is hell, the eternal death of those who die in sin and malicious unbelief.

Pergamum: The Need to Be Countercultural (2:12-17)

As the Word of God, Jesus is a two-edged sword. His word challenges listeners to make up their minds. They must either accept him or reject him. Jesus will not allow them to be indifferent to him or his message. That is the image he shows to the Christians of Pergamum.

Because of a dispute with Egypt, Pergamum was unable to import papyrus. As a result the people of Pergamum developed their own paper industry and created a high quality "Pergama Paper," which we know as parchment. The parchment business made them prosperous and became the source of their library which rivaled that of Alexandria.

Jesus tells the Christians of Pergamum that he knows they live in the sight of "Satan's throne" (verse 13). He is referring to the shrine of Asclepius, a popular healing mecca for people with various illnesses. Near it was an altar dedicated to Zeus, with a series of marble steps rising up to a stage behind which was a vast array of sculptures depicting struggling gods and giants. This altar has been brought by German archaeologists to Berlin and installed inside a museum built especially to house it.

Jesus praises the Pergamum Christians for resisting the temptation to go to the healing shrine or participating in the colorful festivals at the Zeus altar. They remained loyal to Jesus their real healer and true Lord. Moreover, they did not deny their faith when a fellow Christian, Antipas, was executed for his fidelity to Jesus. The martyrdom increased their commitment to Christ.

Still, they were not perfect in the faith. Jesus draws their attention to their confusion about what is good and bad in the culture. They must learn the truth and live by it. From Christ's mouth comes the two-edged sword, the word of true Christian teaching. They have felt pressures from the culture to go to the healing shrine and the Zeus feasts, but happily resisted that.

Nicolaitans and Baalamites — False Teachers

Unfortunately, they were less perceptive when faced with the sexual seductions of the culture and the seemingly innocent eating of food sacrificed to idols. Some Christians argued that the freedom of grace preached by St. Paul meant they were free to practice fornication and adultery and eat the temple meat.

In this passage they are called Nicolaitans and the followers of Balaam — the name of a false prophet in the Old Testament — who advocated sexual immorality and the eating of idolatrous food. The Nicolaitans and Baalamites in Pergamum seemed credible enough. They are ostensible Christians. In fact they are false teachers. They are heretics pretending to present Christ's true teachings, but are calling for accommodation to cultural practices which are non-Christian. They were subverting the church from within. Bad theology will result in un-Christian behavior.

The Sword of Truth — The White Stone of Faith

Jesus awakens them to the untrue teachings of such people. The real Christians must reject such teachings, repent, and be converted from these practices. In addition they should fight against the false teachings with the sword of truth that comes from the lips of Jesus. As a reward, Jesus will give them genuine Christian food, the "hidden manna," which provides eternal life.

He will also give them a white stone on which is written a new name. Pagans were fond of wearing amulets on which were written magical names — something similar to the New Age necklaces popular today. The pagan names were used to tap mysterious powers. Christ would give Christians his name by which alone they acquire the spiritual power needed to be saved.

Thyatira: Beware of Jezebel (2:18-29)

Jesus, the Son of God, focuses his fiery eyes of judgment on Thyatira. Here was a city famed for its clothing industry, its weavers and wool-dyers. Lydia, Paul's first convert in Europe, had been a cloth merchant in Thyatira and went on to do business as a dealer in purple cloth in Philippi (cf. Acts 16:14).

The Seductions of Jezebel

Jesus praised the Christians of Thyatira for their love, faith, service, and endurance. But they had succumbed to the same illusions about sexual immorality and eating temple meat as happened at Pergamum. This time the false teacher is a woman whom Jesus calls Jezebel. This may not be her real name. Calling her Jezebel identifies her with the woman of the Old Testament who advocated idolatry and sexual misconduct (II Kg. 9:22).

The Thyatiran woman styled herself as a prophetess and misled Christians into evil behavior under the guise that it really was acceptable to Christ. After all, redemption had made them "free." Sexual freedom was a gift of Christ, she claimed. In our own time there have been teachers within the church that have developed excuses for sexual libertinism.

Jesus predicts the new Jezebel will suffer the same fate as the woman of old. This will demonstrate that Jesus, with the eyes of fire, is still the "searcher of hearts and minds" (verse 23). Jesus then mentions those who hold the "so-called deep secrets of Satan" (verse 24). Paul had ecstatically praised the deep things of God (Rom. 11:33). False teachers at Thyatira preached complex doctrines which were only superficial. The deep things of Satan were imaginary, like the Genesis Tree of the Knowledge of Good and Evil. Jesus rejoiced that most of his Thyatirans were not taken in by this nonsense.

Jesus promises those, who obey Christian morality, authority over the nations. Obedience to the Christian moral commandments brings true strength and freedom. Only those who obey learn how to command. The loyal ones will receive the "morning star," the gift of Christ himself. (The expression "morning star" refers to the real light of the world, Jesus Christ. The Devil, before his fall, was called Lucifer, whose name is variously translated as Day Star, Morning Star, Light-Bearer. After his fall, he is called "diabolus," a word which means divider. The Devil is the bearer of darkness.)

Reflection

1. How is my love of the Eucharist enhanced by a home Mass?
2. Jesus asked the Ephesians to recover their "first love." What must I do to revive my first love for my spouse, my children, my friends, my relationship to Jesus?
3. How can I increase my patience in the face of pain?

4. How do I react when others cut me down? How should I react?
5. In what ways does the promise of heaven help me cope with my troubles here on earth?
6. What means do I take to resist the culture's message of sexual freedom?
7. How do I help my children or other young people to resist our culture's teaching on sexual immorality?
8. Today's idolatry begins with a "me first" attitude. What helps me to put God first?
9. How do I make sure I follow Christ's real teachings and not those of false prophets in our society?
10. What comparisons have I noted between the churches of Ephesus, Smyrna, Pergamum, and Thyatira and my own church today?

Prayer

Lord Jesus, you revealed yourself in your risen glory and with your fiery eyes of judgment to the first churches. You drew them to true teaching with the two-edged sword of your revelation. All this was meant to encourage their virtues and convert them from behavior at variance with Christianity. Come to me with that same revelation and power that I may grow in an authentic spirituality and proper moral witness. May your Spirit actively make that happen in me.

3 Cultural Christians Vs. Faith Christians

One of the reasons we read history is to learn from the experience of those who came before us. Those who forget history are condemned to repeat it. But when we read Scripture we do more than look at old words and old deeds. Scripture is God's Word that speaks both to the people of biblical times and to us today. We look back to get the feel of the history, culture, and questions of the original events and how Jesus acted and spoke in those situations. We must also treat God's Word as addressing our own needs today. That is the spirit for studying and praying Scripture. In chapter 2 we reviewed the letters sent to four of the seven churches. In this chapter we meditate on the letters to the other three churches.

Sardis: Greed Corrupted This Church (3:1-6)

Jesus appears to Sardis as a judge. That is the meaning of the seven-starred scepter he carries. Situated sixty miles east of Smyrna, the city of Sardis was know for its manufacture of jewelry and the minting of coins. The expression "rich as Croesus" comes from Sardis, for it was here that Croesus made his fortune minting coins.

What is the Christian problem at Sardis? Wealth. Unlike their poor comrades in Smyrna, the church at Sardis bought into the prosperous lifestyle and commerce of this community. Christians made their fortunes on marketing jewels and selling coins. They apparently had no trouble with the Romans, most likely because they purchased protection. Like many a church community ever since, both parishes and monasteries, they succumbed to the temptations of money. They lost the vigor of their faith and shared in the corruption that too much money causes for so many people.

Greed is not friendly to faith. It is the root of virtually every evil. "For the love of money is the root of all evils, and some people in their desire for it have strayed from the faith and have pierced themselves with many pains" (I Tm. 6:10). Of the seven capital sins, avarice corrodes the soul more than the other six. In the gospels, Jesus condemned greed more than any other evil.

This is why he is harsher with the Sardis church more than the others. He calls them the living dead. "I know your works, that you have the reputation for being alive, but you are dead" (verse 1). The most prominent religion at Sardis was the cult of Cybele which claimed the power of raising people from the dead. Jesus reminds his followers that they have accepted the spiritual death of greed. Cybele can neither raise them from physical nor spiritual death. Only Jesus can liberate them from the illusions caused by wealth.

In their baptismal promises they committed themselves to the life of the beatitudes, the first of which called them to poverty of spirit. Jesus commended the few of them who have not soiled their baptismal garments with the dirt of greed. "They will walk with me dressed in white, because they are worthy" (verse 4). He warns those who seem so secure in their possessions that he will come like a "thief in the night," meaning that death will overtake them unexpectedly and then all their acquisitions will mean nothing to them.

They made the great mistake of identifying themselves in terms of what they had instead of discovering who they were, images of God, endowed with intrinsic human dignity. Instead of having the spiritual freedom of the children of God, they were enslaved and deadened by what they owned. This is as true of some Christians today as it was then. The enchantment of avarice corrupts Christians now as always.

But for those — rich or poor — who remain faithful to the person of Jesus and his commands, there will be the prize of the white garment of resurrection and the enrollment of their names in the Book of Life forever (verse 5).

Philadelphia: The Keys of the Kingdom (3:6-13)

Jesus reveals himself to the Philadelphians as one holding the Key of David. The reference to David recalls the fact that this king conquered Rabbah upon whose ruins the city of Philadelphia was built. The builder was Ptolemy Philadelphus. Philadelphia means "love of brother." Some have concluded that this Ptolemy was very fond of his brother and named the city in honor of his affection for him.

This Philadelphia was a gateway city for immigrants and other transients from the east. It was the New York or Ellis Island of its day. Situated over a fault, the city suffered from at least four known earthquakes. Hence the Christians there would share the common insecurity of potential natural disasters as well as the anxiety caused by government hostility.

The citation also remembers the giving of the key of David to the steward Eliakim. He would have exclusive access to the private apartment of the king. Anyone who wanted to reach the king would have to go through him (cf. Is. 22:22 and II Kg. 18:18). The point here is that Jesus alone has the key that enables Christians to enter God's kingdom.

Jesus notes the anxieties of the Christians of Philadelphia. "You have limited strength" (verse 8). Unsettled by the environment and political threats, the church faced an uncertain future. They worried about their families and children. They encountered economic insecurity. Yet, in spite of that, as Jesus declares, they have obeyed the Word of God and did not deny the name of Jesus.

Their world was falling apart but they trusted that Jesus would keep them together. Their faith led them to draw their inner strength from Jesus who held the key to their hopes. The door of despair would not remain closed. Jesus had the key that infused them with hope and opened doors that their precarious situation seemed to hold closed. They had confidence in the sovereignty of Christ. Jesus is the messenger of hope, not a conveyor of despair.

Evangelizers

A second meaning of the "open door" is evangelization. To some extent Jesus asks them to forget their own problems and embark on a joyful sharing of the Gospel. This gateway city was full of people coming and departing. The career change in their lives afforded a perfect opportunity for the local church to reach out to them and share their faith in Jesus Christ.

Sharing the Gospel works best when the preachers are witnesses of what they teach. Pope Paul VI wrote that people today do not listen to teachers. They pay attention to witnesses. If people listen to preachers and teachers, it is because first of all they are witnesses.

Jesus encourages the Philadelphia Christians to be conscious of the persuasive power of their own witness. "You have kept my message of endurance" (verse 10). They were excellent witnesses of the Gospel. The local church should not go through the open door of hope and salvation by themselves. They should reach out and share the kingdom with others and bring them into the life of hope and stability in a changing and threatening world.

Finally, Jesus promises the Philadelphia Christians that he will protect them in the time of trial that will face the whole world. This does not mean they will be spared the pain and anguish of persecution, but that they will succeed in keeping their faith in the fire that "will test the inhabitants of the earth" (verse 10). Christian disciples are expected to carry their crosses and follow Jesus to the end.

Pillars in the Temple of God

As a reward, Christians will become pillars of the church. Earthquakes might tumble the great homes, the factories, and the defensive walls. Pillars often survived earthquakes. The state might uproot the Christian families. But through it all, nothing will shake the faith of those followers of Jesus. The church has a future because the faith-filled are spiritual pillars that are earthquake-proof. The name of Christ will be so deeply inscribed on their souls that the name Christian will survive all efforts to destroy it.

After two thousand years of church history, we have many examples of the glorious faith of our mothers and fathers who stayed committed to Jesus and the church despite all efforts to kill them. They teach us how to trust in Christ. If we imitate them, we will also become the pillars of love for a church against whom even the gates of hell cannot prevail.

Laodicea: Jesus Condemns Lukewarm Believers (3:14-22)

To Laodicea Jesus comes as a great "Amen." Jesus is not a compromiser. He has no theology of compromise. He means what he says and says what he means.

Like Sardis, Laodicea was also a rich community. They marketed a much coveted black wool made from a local breed of sheep. Their embroidered suits and dresses were a major export. They produced a well-known eye medicine known as Phrygian powder. The people liked to buy this ointment to smear on their eyes that they might see (verse 18). Their bankers had branch offices all over the empire.

Here again, as in Sardis, we have a case of a rich Christian community that compromised its faith in order to keep its money. Very likely, these Christians paid the officers of the state to turn a blind eye to their religious affiliation. There was no persecution of the church at that time in Laodicea because the Christians were so limp in their commitment that there was nothing to persecute. They were like everybody else, so why bother singling them out.

Selective Believers

The Christians at Sardis suffered from an acute case of greed. Those at Laodicea were infected with selective belief. They picked those parts of Christ's teaching that suited them and their acceptance in the local society. They were not going to be "fanatics" who received the whole message of Jesus. They ignored those aspects of Christianity that might imperil their wealth or their standing with the pagans around them. They were not "hot" Christians fully devoted to Jesus. Nor were they "cold" Christians giving up their frail attachment to Jesus altogether. They espoused what seemed to them to be a reasonable middle way, a theology of compromise with the culture. They were spiritually corrupt. They were cultural Christians.

Jesus confronts them with their major weakness. "I know that you are neither cold nor hot. I wish you were either cold or hot. So, because you are lukewarm, neither hot or cold, I will spit you out of my mouth" (verses 15-16). The water supply of Laodicea was infamous for its vapid taste, not cold and refreshing nor hot and pure. It was a local joke that the best thing to do with the disgusting water was to spit it out. It was a perfect image of the state of the Christian's lack of spirituality at Laodicea.

In his Sermon on the Mount Jesus had said, "No one can serve two masters. . . . You cannot serve God and mammon" (Mt. 6:24). Mammon means money. Wealth is a demanding master. So is God. One must choose which lord one will obey. At Laodicea the Christians tried the impossible. They loved their money and their social acceptance. They gave up those demands of Christ which impeded their pursuit of money and the praise from the pagans. They tried to serve two masters and failed.

Some prosperous Catholics in today's culture are new "Laodiceans." They select teachings of Christ which do not hinder their acceptance by the culture. They reject those which do. Such Catholics buy the culture's position on birth control, abortion, divorce, homosexuality, social justice, and other moral issues. Polls report that such Catholics are likely to say, "I feel I can disagree with the pope and still be a good Catholic."

Jesus would say to these rich and affluent Catholics just what he said to the Laodiceans. "You are wretched, pitiable, poor, blind, and naked" (verse 17). Jesus does not say this with bitterness or lack of concern for his flock. He speaks with affection, rebuking them in order to bring them to repentance and conversion. "Those, whom I love, I reprove and chastise. Be earnest, therefore, and repent" (verse 19).

People may be indifferent to Jesus, but he is not indifferent to them. His love is always hot. They may be dull with pleasure and economic security. He is ardent with sorrow about the state of their souls. He knocks at the door of each human heart, an image marvelously captured in a world-famous painting by Holman Hunt.

He stands at the door of their hearts and shouts words of love to wake them up and bring them to real personal fulfillment. He begs them to listen. "Whoever has ears ought to hear what the Spirit says to the churches." He continues the struggle of his passion in his mystical Body. Just as he suffered in his earthly life to bring people to the kingdom, so he strives in agony in his mystical life as the risen Lord to save every person while there is time. The result will be the only true source of happiness on earth and in heaven, union with Jesus. "I will enter his house and dine with him, and he with me" (verse 20).

Summary of the Messages to the Seven Churches

The rich teaching of these seven letters deserves a summary review. Following is a grid that will help in seeing the whole situation at a glance. The first column lists the virtue of a given church where there is one. The second column contains the vice of a certain church where one is present. The last column reveals a special reward for the churches that remain faithful to Jesus.

Overview of the Seven Churches

	Virtue	Vice	Reward for Fidelity
Ephesus	Discerns True Teaching	Lost First Love	Will Eat From the Tree of Life
Smyrna	Poor, But Rich in Faith		Crown of Life
Pergamum	Resisted Paganism	Some Ate Idol Food	Hidden Manna
Thyatira	Faith, Love Service	Idol Food Sexual Freedom	Authority Over Nations
Sardis		The Greedy Living Dead	Enrolled in Book of Life
Philadelphia	Never Denied Jesus		Pillars of Church
Laodicea		Greedy Cultural Christians	Will Dine With Jesus

Note that two of the churches, Sardis and Laodicea, are not praised for any virtues. They are the rich churches which have compromised with their cultures. At the same time, see that two of the churches, Smyrna and Philadelphia, are not condemned for having any vices. They also happen to be the poorest of the communities. They are the churches of the first beatitude about poverty of spirit. Wealth has corrupted the rich churches who have compromised their faith.

The virtues and vices of the seven churches can be found in our own church today. The messages to these churches are really to the universal church of every age of history. Writing from his lonely prison on Patmos, John, the vigilant pastor, knows the strengths and weaknesses of those churches clustered near his own church of Ephesus. Inspired by visions from Jesus, he sends his beloved people pastoral letters to call them to renewed faith. He uses imagery that lifts local problems above present circumstances to focus their attention on the final goal of history as well as the ultimate outcome of their personal lives. The remaining chapters of the Book of Revelation will reflect the experience of the end of time with ever more dramatic symbols and pictures.

The seven rewards are not just individually tailored to each church. They are a summary picture of the ultimate prize that will be given to every Christian who remains faithful to Jesus, his person, message, and commands. All those who stay faithful will eat of the tree of life, wear the crown of life, dine on the hidden manna, exercise authority over the nations, be enrolled in the book of life, stand humbly as pillars of the church, and feast with Jesus in the heavenly kingdom.

Today we love process, but think little of goals. The Seven Letters urge us to contemplate both the process of the faith journey and the goal to which it leads us. To concentrate on process alone is to fritter away our lives without purpose. To gaze only at the goal and forget the process is to live in a dream world. Both are needed. Christianity is a challenging religion. The reward goes only to those strong in faith. And that strength comes from trust in — and union with — Jesus Christ, His Spirit, and the Father who calls us.

Reflection

1. What examples of self-destructive greed do I know about?
2. How does the greed of a few cause more poverty in the many?
3. What examples can I give from present or past church history that show how greed negatively affects faith?
4. What seeds of avarice do I see in my own life?
5. How would a modern Catholic deny or betray Jesus?
6. What qualities of character do I need in order to avoid ever denying what my religion demands of me?
7. How would I describe a "cultural Catholic?"
8. What do I think of a Catholic who believes all the church's teachings, but is a sinner, and a Catholic who chooses what he or she wants to believe, and is a sinner?
9. Look at the list of Christ's seven rewards. What does each one tell me about my faith goals?
10. Why is it important both to focus on my faith journey as well as the goals to which I journey?

Prayer

Lord Jesus, you are my beginning and my end. You encompass my whole life. You are behind me, gently urging me forward. You are ahead of me, calling me to my faith goals. You are beside me, holding my hand, lest I falter on the journey. You are in my heart to make me strong. You are outside me to urge me to courageous behavior. To you be honor, glory, and praise now and forever.

4 Heaven Opens

A Mood Change in the Text

Up to this point the Book of Revelation sounds like a normal scriptural text, slightly modified by the special images surrounding Christ. The situation of the seven churches provides a realistic tone. Those Christians witnessed many of the same virtues and were prone to similar vices as found in our church today.

Those churches were in trouble externally from a hostile government and internally from various moral weaknesses. They were not abandoned by God. Christ really cared about them. Jesus, robed in symbols of power and judgment, walked among the "seven lampstands" of the churches, prepared to take on the worldly might of Rome and heal the spiritual frailties of his flock.

From the fourth chapter onward, the text of the Book of Revelation abounds with puzzling symbols, spectacular visions, and a fantastic flow of images. There are wild scene shifts between the joys of heaven and the sorrows of earth. We behold Jesus as a fierce judge before whom evil powers tremble with fear and terror. We see him again as one so beautiful and loveable that songs of ecstasy tumble at his feet from those blessed by him. There is a feeling of a dream because the vividness of the scenes seem unencumbered by ordinary color and constraint.

There Is a Pattern in the Chaos

The progress is like the chaotic flow of lava. There is indeed a pattern of meaning, but it is a wave, not a line. This is not an orderly play in three acts. It is a jumble of divine and human realities thrown together in a seemingly unpredictable mix. It is best to think of it as the waves that wash up on the shore. No wave is exactly like the other. Nor is the timing of each wave's arrival exact and mechanical. Yet the rhythm and the inevitability communicate a satisfying and restful pattern. It assures the ear as well as the eye.

Hence Revelation should be heard as well as seen. Read the words out loud. Only looking at the visions reduces them to a flat canvas where parts can be cut up and then pieced together in an imposed pattern. Hearing the visions gives you the "surrounding," the spiritual environment intended by the author. It would be a mistake to approach this book with a narrow focus. Better to have ears that catch the broad collection of impressions and patterns contained in it.

Scholars call this kind of writing the "apocalyptic style." Apocalypse means revelation. But since all of the Bible is revelation, that definition does not help much. Apocalypse is revelation with a difference. It is a subdivision of prophecy. The prophets of the Bible had three purposes: (1) To purify God's people from their sins by appealing to God's law and human conscience; (2) To predict — with assurance — the coming of the Messiah and a messianic age. This meant that God would accomplish his purposes in history; (3) To interpret the signs of the times, that is, to help people see what God wanted of them in a given period of history. When the times seemed absolutely chaotic and dangerous beyond any living memory, the prophets used apocalyptic language to interpret them.

When Was Apocalyptic Talk Used?

Now there are three special historical moments in the Bible that were so filled with crisis and threat that the prophets resorted to catastrophe language to interpret the signs of those dreadful days. When a house is on fire, we do not calmly speak of vacation plans. We yell about the danger. So did the prophets.

The first was the Babylonian seventy-year captivity of the Jews, about six centuries before Christ. The second was the time of the public ministry of Jesus when the conflict between Jerusalem and Rome neared its tragic showdown. The third was the beginning of the Roman persecution of Christians near the end of the first century of the Christian era.

Examples of prophets using the apocalyptic style correspond to each era. Ezekiel and Daniel prophesy to the discouraged Babylonian captives. The Last Judgment sermons of Jesus — in his prophetic role — are addressed to Jerusalem on a collision course with Rome. John's Book of Revelation speaks to the suffering church at the end of the first century.

Ezekiel, Daniel, Jesus, and John freely speak of falling suns, bloody moons, massive deaths, wars, earthquakes, famine, disease, hunger, pain, unchecked cruelties, knives, blood, and all the other negative power words. They also paint cosmic processions in which God makes a grand visible entrance onto the world scene. Trumpets, choirs, shouts, organs, drums, and all the imposing conqueror images accompany the mighty and victorious God. The purpose is to call people to hope and trust in God's power to overcome evil. Believers should never surrender to fear and despair. Epic times need epic talk to describe them. That is what apocalyptic language does.

A Worship Service in Heaven (4:1-11)

Sometimes things get so bad on earth the only place we can turn to is heaven. John walks along the beaches of Patmos brooding about the difficulties of the church. Then the clouds of history's problems parted and John saw the door of heaven opened. God invited him to an experience of heaven. It was a moment of sheer joy. "At once I was caught up in spirit" (verse 2).

John beheld God's throne. God sparkled like a jewel. A rainbow framed the throne. Early in scriptural history, God had told Noah that he would place a rainbow stretching from sky to earth to symbolize his desire for a union between heaven and earth. Divine love sought intimacy with people. God wanted to be close to his beloved church.

Twenty-four elders sat on lesser thrones around God. These represented the twelve patriarchs of Israel, the first People of God, and the twelve apostles who represented the new People of God. They wore the white robes of priesthood, because it was their duty to bridge any gulf between God and the human family. The word priest comes from a term meaning bridge-builder. The crowns on their heads spoke of their authority, meaning their responsibility to author a growth of loving union between the human and the divine.

Lightning and thunder emanate from the throne. Throughout Scripture, these elements of an electric storm are always associated with a revelation of the divine presence. A clap of thunder and a bolt of lightning still stir up awe even in our technological age. Because we are so insulated from nature, we do not follow our feeling of awe and let it lead us to thoughts of God. But for the ancients, nakedly exposed to nature's awesome displays, the force of nature easily awoke an awareness of God.

Pagans identified God with nature itself and so invented nature gods. Biblical people believed in a personal God, one who was God of the storm, not the storm itself. In this scene the flashes of fire and peals of thunder signal to John that he would be privileged to experience God directly.

Seven archangels, the "seven spirits of God," illumined the scene like torches. It was one such "fire angel" who had touched the lips of the prophet Isaiah and conveyed to him God's purification of his sinfulness (cf. Is. 6). The sea of crystal-like glass which constituted the floor of heaven evoked in John the feeling of the serenity of God, the ultimate fullness of peace that is our final destiny. All the strident dissonance that tears at human nerves because of conflict, hatred, envy, ambition, and wars yields in heaven to a harmony based on the perfect reconciliation of God and humans — and of humans to one another.

At the very center of the throne room stand four creatures "covered with eyes in front and in back" (verse 6). The eyes here stand for insight more than mere visual ability. This is a spiritual event more than a physical one. Sight views a body. Insight understands the heart. Sight ponders the flow of events. Insight uncovers their meaning. Sight notices a church. Insight reveres the God of the church.

One creature resembled a lion, another an eagle, the next an ox, and the last one a man. These same four creatures may be seen in Ezekiel 1:4-21. It is a curious fact that the Book of Revelation never quotes the Old Testament, yet every chapter is full of images borrowed from it. St. Irenaeus of Lyon was the first one to apply these images to the authors of the four gospels. Matthew is the Man, Mark the Lion, Luke the Ox, and John the Eagle.

Hence the gospels and the four evangelists are the center of heaven's throne room, for they reveal the essential will of God. God's Word has the nobility of a lion, the strength of an ox, the wisdom of a man, and the soaring mobility of an eagle. The gospels proclaim that God loved us so much that he sent us Jesus to save us and bring us eventually to the happiness and glory of communion with God.

Now all the participants of the heavenly liturgy are in place: God on his throne; the twenty four elders; the seven angels; the four evangelists. Let the liturgy of heaven begin."Holy, holy, holy is the Lord God almighty!" (verse 8). The patriarchs and apostles lay their crowns on the floor before God, creatures joyfully acknowledging their creator. Down on earth, the King of Persia had laid his crown at the feet of Nero and said, "Our lord and god." Domitian and Tiberius let themselves be called god. The heavenly scene teaches us there is only one God and that creatures will find their supreme fulfillment in committing themselves to the real God.

Reflection

1. How am I reacting to all these symbols in Revelation?
2. Why do Ezekiel, Daniel, Jesus, and John use "apocalyptic talk"?
3. How deep is my faith in God's involvement in history?
4. Read Revelation 4 out loud. What difference do you notice from just reading it silently?
5. When you hear the word prophet, what do you think is the prophet's job?
6. Who are some modern people referred to as prophets? Why have they been so named?
7. Why are prophets often disliked?
8. The biblical rainbow first appeared after the Flood. It appears again in Revelation. Why does it symbolize the reconciliation of God and people?
9. We hear thunderclaps in this chapter. How does thunder affect you? What is its purpose in the Book of Revelation?
10. What is the purpose of the four symbols of the gospels in this vision?

Prayer

Gracious God, you lift us from earth to heaven to behold the eternal liturgy of joy. Help us to realize that the litany we attend at our parish church is a reflection of this ceremony of praise, joy, and peace. Enable our faith to see beyond our earthly experiences to the eternal reality of heaven itself.

5 The Lamb Appears

The Revelation of the Lamb (5:1-14)

During his second pastoral visit to the United States, Pope John Paul II attended an ecumenical service in the football stadium of the state university in Columbia, South Carolina. Some had objected to raising a cross on state property, until the actual moment of the pope's arrival. The planners of the event developed a beautiful way to do this. While fifty thousand people sang the stirring hymn, "When I Survey the Wondrous Cross," five men emerged from the end zone opposite the stage at the other end. They carried a large wooden cross in a horizontal position.

Parallel to them another group of men bore an enormous banner — also in a horizontal position — on which was woven the image of the Lamb that was slain and risen from the dead. As the great congregation sang the final words of the hymn, the men simultaneously planted the cross and the banner of the Lamb in front of the stage exactly at the moment the pope arrived. The exaltation of the cross and the victory of the Lamb, and the appearance of the pope perfectly captured the religious faith and emotion of that moment. That event gives us some sense of what John experienced when he was privileged to behold the revelation of the Lamb as he describes it in the beginning of chapter 5.

The heavenly music subsided and all eyes were on God who held up a scroll in his right hand. There was writing on both sides of the scroll and it was secured with seven seals. We are so accustomed to an avalanche of paper and buildings full of books that we forget what it was like in a culture where paper was scarce and a scroll was a luxury. Only the rich and the powerful could afford to own scrolls, and not many of them at that. Focusing on the scroll signified the importance of the message at hand.

Often the message on the scroll was written on both sides just in case one side might become damaged. Scrolls were used for legal documents, palace histories and religious writings, such as the Bible itself. Egyptian papyrus and Pergamum parchment were the papers of choice. The scroll in God's hand contained his message about the future of history and the final coming of Jesus Christ.

John heard an angel ask who was worthy to open the scroll. No one answered. John found himself overwhelmed with tears. Was the future to remain obscure? Would no one tell him the outcome both of present sorrow and of history itself? An elder consoled him and advised him to stop weeping. "The lion of the tribe of Judah, the root of David, triumphed, enabling him to open the scroll" (verse 5). These messianic images refer to Jesus.

Why the Lamb?

Then John beheld Jesus as the Passover Lamb, the Lamb that had been slain but now is risen and victorious over death. The Book of Revelation would speak of Jesus as Lamb twenty-eight times. Why this emphasis on the symbolism of a lamb? The People of God in the Old Testament appeared first as nomadic shepherds. The lamb was essential to their economy and livelihood providing food for the table and wool for their clothing. A lamb meant a lot to them.

They used the lamb to express their spiritual dependence on God. A lamb was their central sacrificial offering. By the command of God, the blood of a lamb was smeared on their door posts in Egypt to save their firstborn from the avenging angel. The lamb was the centerpiece of their most important supper, the annual Passover Meal which recalled their deliverance from Egypt. In the gospels Jesus is often called the lamb of God. Jesus personalized the meaning of the lamb. As Son of God become flesh, Christ could accomplish a sacrifice never possible for an animal. At the ninth hour on Good Friday, the High Priest sacrificed the last lamb and pronounced the liturgical word, "Kalah" (meaning "It is finished"). At Calvary Jesus looked at his own body, the true lamb of God, and said, "Kalah — It is finished."

This is the rich religious and cultural background for the use of lamb imagery in Revelation. The lamb symbolizes deliverance from evil and redemption from sin. Whereas the lamb in other books of the Bible moves toward the altar of sacrifice and the battle with evil, in Revelation the lamb is victorious. The sacrifice is over. The process of making the victory felt in all creation and history is underway.

Jesus appeared in the heavenly throne room bearing many of the images we have already seen. He has the seven eyes of divine insight into the hearts of people. The seven archangel messengers are ready to bring his Word to all creation. He received the scroll from his Father and then was adored by the twelve patriarchs and twelve apostles. Gold vessels, filled with charcoal and incense, emitted clouds of aromatic smoke, a visible expression of the prayers of God's holy people. Harp music accompanied an outburst of song praising Jesus for his redemptive works. "Worthy are you to receive the scroll . . . with your blood you purchased for God those from every tribe and tongue" (verse 9).

The intensity of music swells as all the inhabitants of heaven, countless in number, add their voices to praise Jesus. Finally, every man and woman on earth, along with all the birds of the air, the fish of the sea and the beasts of the forests join their voices in a third chorus that expresses boundless love for Jesus who has shown them such magnificent affection. The gospel writers finish the hymn with a determined, "Amen." Everyone bows in adoration before Jesus Christ.

Chapters 4 and 5 provide a liturgical setting for the teachings that are to follow. Doctrine is proclaimed in the middle of the glory of worship. There is an old Catholic Latin saying that fits here. "Lex orandi est lex credendi." (The law of praying is the law of believing.) Our prayers, readings, gestures, processions, and songs at liturgy are expressions of our faith teachings or doctrines.

Doctrine alone can seem abstract, dry, and sometimes unconvincing. At liturgy, our Catholic teaching is prayed in an environment of faith, feeling, color, candlelight, aromatic incense, sculpture, architecture, paintings and sacred movements such as hands upraised, signs of the cross, processions, and peace gestures. Liturgy makes us experience doctrine as a spiritual contact with the presence of God.

The great worship scene in chapters 4 and 5 teach us that doctrine should not just be taught in classrooms, but also experienced in a community caught up in the faith events of liturgy. It also tells us that our earthly worship is a reflection of divine worship in heaven. More accurately, when we are at a Eucharistic celebration, for example, the heavenly liturgy is present at our earthly one.

The angels and the elders and the choirs of heaven lie behind our own music and prayers. God, the One who sits upon the throne, is there. Jesus, the victorious Lamb, is there. The gospels at the center of the throne room are there. In a very real way, our participation in the liturgy of our local parish church is already a beginning of our sharing in the liturgy of heaven. In a sense, these are practice sessions for eternal life. For the suffering Christians of John's time, the splendor of the heavenly liturgy as the hidden reality of their simple house Eucharists was a great consolation to them.

Reflection

1. Which images in chapters 4 and 5 affect me most?
2. How real is heaven to me? Is it a practical goal of my life?
3. Why is the lamb an excellent image of Jesus?
4. What music do I know that reminds me of the hymns in Revelation?
5. Why is it important that I pray my faith doctrine at worship?
6. How often do I think of heaven's presence at earthly worship?
7. What are three reasons why I should worship God?
8. If I lived in biblical times when paper was scarce and expensive, what impact would that have on me? Why would a scroll seem so important?
9. What three books do I treasure most? Why?
10. What would be missing in my life if I did not worship God?

Prayer

Worthy are you, O Jesus, to receive praise, honor, and glory always. You have always been motivated by perfect love in all that you did in becoming a man and ministering to the poor, the sick, the needy, and the sinful. You came to the suffering church of the first century to give them hope when despair seemed the only option. Please come to us today when we need a new infusion of hope in a time of confusion and uncertainty. Reveal your glory again as you did to the first believers. Bring heaven closer to earth that your eternal joy may be experienced today.

6 The Four Horsemen Are Coming

Who's in Charge?

In a bloody battle scene in Francis Ford Coppola's film, *Apocalypse Now*, a messenger wanders into the front lines. Dazed by the chaos, he asks, "Who's in charge here?" No one answers his question. History is full of periods of confusion, war, famine, terror, and conflict. It makes people wonder if anyone is in charge.

Who's in charge? In the eighteenth century, the Enlightenment philosophers declared that human beings have taken control of the world and God had become an amiable and powerless chairman of the board. The human masters of control said they were in charge. In our century they gave us two world wars, the holocaust, the Cambodian killing fields, and the rape of the rain forests in Brazil.

Revelation's answer is that God is in charge of the world and the outcome of history. God gave men and women freedom. They could either make a hell of life on earth, or, with God's grace, make it a place of love, justice, and mercy. Without God, we see what we have done with history. In all other times, these tragedies were occasions for conversion and repentance. They still are, only the voices of Christianity must be raised to issue the call. God is in charge, but he requires our grace-assisted cooperation to move the world toward a positive goal of harmony and reconciliation.

This viewpoint should govern our understanding of the catastrophes John introduces at this point of the narrative. The lamb proceeds to open the seven seals. The event that follows the opening of each seal refers both to an experience in John's time as well as to the end of the world. We can identify the historical connection with biblical times. We have no certain way of saying that a given event in our own day is a sure sign of the Last Judgment.

Every age has the four horsemen of war, ethnic strife, famine, and death. We have had perhaps the worst examples in history of such things. Yet the end of the world did not occur. With the coming of the year 2000 there will be a lot of end-of-the-world talk. The end of Soviet communism and the restoration of Israel are thought by some to be evidence that Jesus is about to return again.

This is pure speculation based on a literalist interpretation of the text and a pre-conceived notion of how the end will happen. We simply do not know. What we do know is that the trials of history and daily life are invitations to faith, conversion, and repentance. We should approach each day we live as though it were our last. We should not engage in futile searches for exact fulfillment of apocalyptic prophecies. Our energy will be better spent improving the world and our spiritual and moral lives.

The White Horse of War (6:1-2)

The Lamb opens the first seal. It reveals a man on a white horse. The Lamb says, "Come." Bearing the bow of war, the horseman plunges forth, bent on conquest. Some have mistakenly thought the man was Jesus. They confuse this text with Revelation 19:11-12 which tells of a rider on a white horse, whose name is faithful and true. That is clearly Christ. But here the rider is a military figure, carrying the bow of war. The context is a list of woes that will assail the world. The man on the white horse here is not Jesus.

Historically, John may have been thinking of the shocking defeat of the Roman army by the Parthians in A.D. 62. The victorious Parthians, riding their famous white horses, would have held up their bows in triumph. More wars were to come. They would cause suffering for the Christians, along with everyone else. The Romans who were currently causing so much trouble for Christians would them-selves face judgment for their cruelty.

The Red Horse of Ethnic Strife (6:3-4)

The second horse is the color of blood. Its rider will take peace away from the earth, this time in the form of ethnic strife and revolutions. John knew well the sad outcome of the abortive revolutions, which the Jews mounted against Rome and the amount of blood that was shed in the streets. He prophesied that this will increase in the near future of his own time and in the last days.

If we look at our own times and think of the blood that was shed or is being shed between Catholics and Protestants in Belfast, in Beirut between Christians and Moslems, in South Africa between whites and blacks, in Cambodia between the Khmer Rouge and their helpless countrymen, in Yugoslavia between Serbs and Croats, in Azerbaijan between Armenians and Azeris — the list seems endless — we might be prompted to think the last days are upon us. But as Jesus reminds us, "Of that day and hour no one knows . . . but the Father alone" (Mt. 24:36).

The Black Horse of Famine and Economic Crisis (6:5-6)

Now appears the black horse whose rider carries a scale, much like shopkeepers used to weigh food for customers. John hears a voice say, "A ration of wheat costs a day's pay, and three rations of barley costs a day's pay. But do not damage the olive oil or the wine" (verse 6). Where there are food shortages due to famine, crop failure, or inability to deliver the food to the cities, the prices rise. Inflation results. Economic crisis causes all to suffer, the rich who buy wheat and the poor who usually purchase barley.

John prophesies that this will happen when the judgment is made upon those who harass Christians. And this will be one of the major signs that precede the end of the world and the arrival of the Last Judgment. Poverty and hunger will reach an all-time high.

The voice says the oil and the wine will not be damaged. Vines and olive trees have roots that are deeper and so withstand the natural disasters that afflict corn, wheat, and barley crops. Symbolically, the oil and wine refers to the rich whose resources tide them through hard times. Grinding poverty thus lives alongside of immense wealth. Today, rich nations are islands of wealth in a world that has whole continents of poverty. In John's time there were many famines, but Nero and his cronies had plenty of money to buy what was available. The same is true today. Then as now, the gifts of nature are used for the luxury of the few at the expense of the many.

The Pale Horse of Plague and Death (6:7-8)

Lastly, came the pale green horse of plague and death. In the fifteenth century, Albrecht Dürer depicted this scene as Father Time — a thin, bearded judge carrying a three-pronged spear. He is riding at full gallop toward people whose upturned faces look at him with defenseless horror.

In our own time, the Japanese artist Fugita painted the fourth horseman as a skeleton, laughing wildly, riding on the skeleton of a horse across a battlefield strewn with skeletons. A green chlorine cloud of death floats over the scene. Fugita remembers Hiroshima and Nagasaki and uses them to describe this scene from Revelation.

John foresees widespread, violent death caused by plague as another judgment against the sinful who would destroy Christ's kingdom. No person or nation can escape the consequences of sin. "The wages of sin is death" (Rom. 6:23). Sexual promiscuity brings diseases of the flesh. Greed may fill bank accounts, but it empties the soul. Anger that leads to murder also leads to death row. Sloth results in spiritual laziness and dead lives. The sinner incurs the self-destruction that results from sin.

The Fifth Seal: The Tears of the Martyrs (6:9-11)

The Lamb opens the fifth seal and reveals a scene beneath an altar in heaven. We see the souls of the martyrs who were slaughtered because of their faithful witness to Jesus. They wear the white robe of spiritual victory and ask Jesus when he will sit in judgment and "avenge" their blood. This cannot be revenge because that would be contrary to the teaching of Jesus. What they plead for is the restoration of justice in the world and the liberation of Christianity.

They are "beneath the altar." This has two meanings. The heavenly altar images the earthly altars of sacrifice where blood-life was poured out as an offering to God. Christianity no longer has animal sacrifices, but it does have living sacrifices as evidenced in the death of Jesus and the martyrs. We are called to take the cross. We may not be blood martyrs, but we should be "white martyrs," that is, Christians willing to consecrate our lives to sacrificial love for the salvation of the world.

The second meaning refers to the practice of the early Christians who turned the graves of martyrs into altars as can be seen today in the Roman catacombs. This is why relics of saints are embedded in the altars of our parish churches.

The World Falls Apart at the Seams (6:12-17)

The Lamb has heard the cry of the martyrs and answers them in the vision unfolded by the sixth seal. It reveals five pictures which every Jew expected would accompany the Day of the Lord and the end of the world.

1. *Earthquake.* One prophet after another foresaw the world falling apart when God comes to judge the earth. "On that day there shall be a great shaking. . . . Mountains shall be overturned and cliffs shall tumble, and every wall shall fall to the ground" (Ez. 38:19, 20).

2. *Sun and Moon Darkened.* "The stars . . . send forth no light; The sun is dark when it rises, and the light of the moon does not shine" (Is. 13:10).

3. *Stars Fall.* Nothing makes us more nervous than when the reliability of the earth fails. Biblical people feared that. So do we. Think of our anxiety over the hole in the ozone layer causing cancer-inducing violet rays to attack our skin. The regularity of the heavens is a sign of God's abiding fidelity. Without that we have chaos. When the stars fall, the end is coming.

4. *A Torn Sky.* Biblical people imagined the sky as a solid dome. Above it was the "third heaven," where God lived. The dome itself was the second heaven. The sun, moon, stars, and clouds were in the atmosphere of the first heaven. Ripping open the dome — tearing apart the sky — meant that God was coming from the third heaven

through the opening to judge the world.

5. *Moveable Mountains.* The most solid thing biblical people (including us) could imagine were mountains. Jesus said faith could move a mountain. Before the Last Judgment the last sign of earthly stability would be taken away. Every mountain would be moved from its place.

All these images can be found in the Old Testament prophets. Jesus used the same pictures in his Last Judgment sermon. The opening of the seals disclosed well-known images and expectations.

What will happen next?

First, the captains and the kings, the rich and powerful, will be scared. No knife, gun, bomb, Swiss bank account will protect them against the judgment. At the same time, the slave and free will also be frightened. All people will be subject to the judgment.

Secondly, everyone will hide. After their sin, what was the first act of the first sinners, Adam and Eve? They hid from God. Sinners do not dread death most. They dread the presence of God. The sinner is a fugitive. Fear and flight mark the behavior of the sinner.

Thirdly, they flee the anger of the Lamb. Usually, the lamb is thought to be sweet and gentle. Here, Jesus as Lamb is the God of wrath. But his anger is not vindictive. It is a wrath born of love to save people. I have said that sinners produce their own self-destruction. Christ the judge confirms what sinners have brought on them-selves. But Jesus wants conversion and repentance. These seals — signs before the end — offer sinners one last chance to change before the end.

What impact can these six seals opened by the Lamb have upon our spiritual lives? What do war, strife, famine, death, the tears of martyrs, and ecological catastrophes teach us for our moral lives?

1. *We have time to change before the end.* Always remember that these signs are not about the actual end of the world, but are events that precede it. We should see them as invitations to take stock of our moral and spiritual lives, of our relationship with Jesus Christ. We could make a case that everyone of the signals found in the six seals are present today. We cannot conclude that they certainly prophesy the end of the "late, great planet earth." But they do give us pause.

No matter what happens, death is coming for all of us, whether in end-of-the-world disasters, or in what normally occurs. Rarely will any one of us say, "Well, I'm going to die, so I will just sit back and let it happen." No. We go to our doctors, take medicine, and try to restore our health. The same is true of the spiritual and moral life. We should get our souls in order, not just before dying, but so that our daily life will have the kind of joyful fulfillment Jesus wants us to have. Just as we have time to change before the end of our personal lives, so we have the same opportunity before the end of the world. It is idle to speculate whether we have reached the end of history. It is not useless to take charge of our lives now and make something of them with the grace of the Holy Spirit.

2. *Think of Jesus as risen and victorious.* Who is the real Jesus now? Is he the baby of Bethlehem? Is he the torn victim on the cross? No. That is part of his earthly history and possesses great power to motivate us to better living. But the real Jesus now is the one risen from the dead. Yes, he continues to embody the grace of the Incarnation which we celebrate at Christmas. Indeed, he still carries the scars of the cross upon his glorified body. But the Jesus who approaches us to love us, save us, and bring us to glory is the Easter Lord of heaven and earth and of all of history. His kingdom has already begun on earth despite the counter-evidence of war, strife, hunger, death, and ecological disasters.

We have a two-thousand-year-old history of saints and martyrs, a magnificent list of love's victories. Heroic parents and virtuous children in every age tell us that Jesus is alive and is Lord. The survival of the church despite every effort of the most hostile forces is clear proof that Jesus has risen from the dead and wants to give us right now the fruits of joyful, heavenly living. That is why he appears as the victorious Lamb in Revelation. Trust in his power for profound personal change.

3. *Experience your need for Jesus Christ.* In the secular mentality of our day, the response to pain, tragedy, and death is one of despair. Some say we should hire a doctor to help us kill ourselves. Doctor-assisted suicide is their answer. Others escape pain in drugs, alcohol, and sex. Some say we should find comfort in blaming others for the ills that besiege us. They push us to blame abusive parents, or the insensitivity of some church leaders, or the

evil behavior of some politicians or financial moguls. A few advise us to grit our teeth and tough it out. There is not much hope in any of this. There is no life, no love, no excitement about the future, no real growth.

All these substitutes remind us that we do want something to heal the ache in our hearts caused by pain, tragedy, and death. God has always understood our need for hope and meaning. He loved us so much he wanted to give us the best answer to these intractable human woes. He did not treat us as a problem to be solved, but a mystery to be loved. He answered us by giving us himself through Jesus Christ. The frightening revelations in the opening of the seals were not meant to scare us and give us even more fear. They were meant to open us to love, which can only be known best in a union with the person of Jesus.

The overwhelming horrors inside the seals are actually a dose of spiritual realism. They are not brought on us by God, but by our own sinfulness. Jesus says, "Look at them. Look at what you have done to yourselves. But, lift up your hearts. I will come to you. I will love you and save you from all of this."

Thank you, Lord Jesus. Come into our lives as fast as you can.

Reflection

1. What is my first impression of the calamities that occur when the seals are opened by the Lamb?
2. When I see similar catastrophes in my own time, what do they reveal to me about God's plan for the world today?
3. How should I respond to people who believe such disasters foretell the imminent end of our world?
4. The martyrs ask Jesus when he will "avenge our blood." How would I interpret this in a Christian way?
5. What calamities of nature make us think of God and judgment?
6. Mountains are images of stability. What other nature images communicate the feeling of reliability and stability?
7. Why should I focus on a Jesus who is victorious and risen?
8. How can catastrophes become a spiritual benefit to me?

9. When have I experienced a need for Jesus to be near me?
10. What are the similarities between the end of the world and the end of my world in death?

Prayer

Victorious Lamb of God, you live to bring me hope and salvation. In the midst of life's troubles, you offer me the opportunity for conversion and repentance. Help me to perceive the spiritual opportunities you offer me in life's setbacks. Rescue me from panic and fear. Fill me with hope and trust. Enable me to see your loving plan in my life and in my world.

7 Joyful, Joyful, We Adore Thee

Everyday wisdom says it is darkest just before the dawn. But it helps to get a glimpse of the dawn so we will be brave in the darkness. Jesus shared the glory of his Transfiguration with Peter, James, and John just before his passion to help them hold onto their faith in him. John remembered that privileged moment at Mount Tabor and the psychological boost it gave him. So now he offers us a vision of the glory of the elect that will occur after the great tribulations he has just described in the opening of the first six seals.

God Marks the Foreheads of Those He Saves (7:1-8)

In biblical thinking, God put angels in charge of the forces of nature. Angels regulated the winds, the waters, and the fires. Popular piety called them the angels of service. They belonged to the lowest order of angels because they never got time off. They did not rest on the sabbath as did observant Jews and Christians. In this scene, God orders the angels in charge of the winds to restrain them until the ceremony of marking out the saved took place. Winds, so often the cause of hurricanes, tornadoes, and carriers of unbearable desert heat, were symbols of destruction and of divine retribution.

Up to this point we have been looking at seals that enclosed the scrolls of tribulation. Now we look at a seal in a positive sense. It will not be a destructive sign, but a saving one. The six seals of death recede from our awareness. The seal of life takes center stage. An angel comes from the East with the seal of life. That great giver of light and life, the sun, rises in the East. When the Magi came to Jesus at the Epiphany, they testified that they had seen a star in the East which led them to Christ.

The angel carries the seal of the living God. Every culture

possesses some symbol which stands for ownership and authority. Even today we notarize documents, not just with a witnessed signature before an approved notary, but also with the notary's embossed seal. In biblical times, kings used the seal from their rings to stamp their possessions as their own. The angel bears the seal of the living God to stamp the foreheads of all human beings who will be God's own people in the coming glory.

John emphasizes the *living reality* of the true God to contrast him with all the false gods of his culture. Prophets had fought with Israel to give up any attraction to gods made of stone or metal in which there was no life. Moses had scourged his people for worshiping a calf made of gold. Why worship a dead thing? In our own times we have abundant evidence of people still trying to get happiness from things. A person may love a thing, but the thing will never love back. The only true joy comes from a wholesome and holy relationship with a living and loving human being — and above all with a living God. We should always identify with the psalmist who sings, "Athirst is my soul for God, the living God!" (Ps. 42:3).

This angel gave strict orders to those in charge of the winds to restrain them until the elect were stamped with the sign of God's loving ownership. In the early church, one of the most solemn ceremonies was the sealing of the baptized after the immersion in the waters. They had put on their new, white baptismal robes and came forward to have the holy oil marked on their foreheads. Now they truly belonged to Jesus. The Holy Spirit of love also possessed their hearts. They heard these words at this moment, "Do not grieve the holy spirit of God, with which you were sealed for the day of redemption" (Eph. 4:30).

Why 144,000?

How many were sealed with God's saving love? John uses the number 144,000. It is a multiple of 12 x 12 x 1000. John is thinking of those who will be saved in his own day as well as in the whole history of salvation. The number refers to completeness, to the perfect number of all who will actually be saved. It is not to be taken literally as though only 144,000 will be saved.

Though John goes on to speak of the numbers in terms of the twelve tribes of Israel, he is not talking about the old Israel. John is teaching about the new Israel, the church. The numbers will include saved Jewish Christians. They also embrace all the saved gentile Christians.

The angel marks their foreheads. A remnant of this custom remains today on Ash Wednesday when Catholics are marked on the forehead with ashes to remind them of their mortality, of their belonging to Christ, and of their commitment to remain faithful to the Gospel. It is a ceremonial reminder of belonging to God.

The Saved From All Nations (7:9-17)

The Lord now gives John a vision of the community of the redeemed. Men and women from every nation, race, people, and tongue, in countless numbers, have been given the loving, possessive mark of Christ on their foreheads. They wear the white robe, a symbol of spiritual victory, and carry a palm branch which is a sign of spiritual triumph. They do not take the credit for this glorious outcome. They sing, "Salvation comes from our God, who is seated upon the throne, and from the Lamb" (verse 10).

Just before his Ascension, Jesus met with the eleven apostles on a lonely mountaintop. Despite their small number and their unpromising talents, Jesus commanded them to conquer the world with the Gospel. He gave them the great commission to go to every nation, preaching the Gospel, baptizing those who come in faith and teaching them to observe what he had commanded (cf. Mt. 28:16-20). The apostle John is now privileged to foresee the outcome of that extraordinary command. In human terms it seemed impossible. With the power of Jesus it is indeed possible.

Two thousand years later we see that the Gospel is now being preached in virtually every country on earth. Millions accept it. Millions reject it. Millions have not yet heard it. Pope John Paul II is excited about yet a greater evangelizing than we have known to this point. He has traveled to the ends of the earth to dramatize Christ's missionary concern. He sees there are so many more to be reached.

"The number of those who do not know Christ and do not belong to the church is constantly on the increase. Indeed, since the end of the Council, it has almost doubled. When we consider this immense portion of humanity which is loved by the Father for whom he sent his Son, the urgency of the church's mission is obvious. . . . Peoples everywhere, open your doors to Christ! (*The Mission of the Redeemer*, 3).

Washed in the Blood of the Lamb

The angels then praise the various qualities of God by which this salvation of so many was accomplished. After this an elder explains how these people came to be saved. "These are the ones who have survived the time of great distress. They have washed their robes and made them white in the blood of the Lamb" (verse 14).

Blood makes us moderns think of death. Blood made biblical people think of life. We advert to the blood loss that results in death. They focused on the role of blood as life-giving. They offered the blood of a lamb to God as a religious gift, a sacrifice. The purpose was twofold, to honor God and undergo a spiritual transformation. That is why sacrifice also included the burning of the lamb. Fire transforms what it burns and the smoke of the sacrifice rises to the third heaven, to God's throne.

New Testament Christians believed that the blood of Christ signified both death and life, a death on the cross in which his blood flowed forth from his body, a source of life in that his blood made new life available to them. Sacramentally, they celebrated this in the Bread and Wine — Body and Blood of Jesus — at Eucharist. The fire now is the grace of the Holy Spirit, won for us by Jesus, and able to change us into disciples of the Lord. The result is moral and spiritual renewal evidenced by repentance and conversion.

The Seventh Seal: Thirty Minutes of Silence in Heaven

"When he broke open the seventh seal, there was silence in heaven for about half an hour" (Rev. 8:1).

We draw back now from the ultimate celebration of the saints, back to the realities of history, both John's, our own, and that of the end of the world. The prayers of the suffering church of all ages beat against heaven's door. But God is silent. The half hour of silence in heaven symbolizes those times in our lives when God withdraws from us the sense of his presence. The Lord seems deaf to our prayers. Our souls are in a desert, throats dry from prayer, hearts aching for a touch of divine presence.

But God is listening. The prayers of the just have penetrated the throne. An angel gathers them into a giant golden censer. Our prayers are the sweet incense placed upon the coals. The angel of fire lights the coals. Then . . . "The smoke of the incense along with the prayers of the holy ones went up before God from the hand of the angel" (8:4). God heard the prayer and instructed the angel to take the burning coals of the censer and pour them on the earth. This broke the silence as the angel hurled plagues on the earth against those who were making Christians suffer. "There were peals of thunder, rumblings, flashes of lightning, and an earthquake" (8:5).

The plagues against the persecutors of Christians were like those against Pharaoh. Just as the ten plagues in Egypt caused the liberation of Jews from Pharaoh, so these new plagues instigated the liberation of Christians from their persecutors.

Bergman's Seventh Seal

Swedish film director Ingmar Bergman took this image and created a film about the Black Plague in medieval Scandinavia. The opening scene shows a quiet dove hovering in the sky. Ominous silence signals trouble. Next we see a crusader, just returned from the Holy Land, walking along a beach. He finds a world ravaged by the Black Plague. He meets death, dressed as a skeletal Father Time, on the beach. The knight plays chess with death. They come to a draw. This allows the knight a reprieve. He will have time to journey to his home and see how his family is doing.

The knight travels through a land marked with universal terror. In taverns and meadows he watches people eat, drink, and be merry in a desperate attempt to deny the coming doom. He sees witches burned in the hope of stopping the terror. He hears fiery sermons about the disease of the national soul that has brought on the wrath of God. Religious penitents roam the streets, scourging their bodies, hoping thereby to avert God's wrath. They hope their processions and chants will inspire everyone to do penance and ward off the anger of God and bring an end to the plague.

Penance abounds, but so does sin. Rape, murder, arson, witch burning, looting, and general debauchery appear everywhere. Extreme behavior occupies center stage in that apocalyptic time. Only a juggler's family offers a single ray of hope and grace. The juggler's name is Joseph. His wife's name is Mary. Their child is Michael, whose name means, "Who is like God?" It is the holy family. They do not participate in the excesses of the age. They neither morbidly whip themselves, nor do their gulp every last ounce of pleasure. The juggler is playful and takes a wondrous view of life. He and his wife and child grieve about the evils of the age and they help people wherever they can.

The knight, however, finds them to be the exception. Everywhere he turns he finds radical anxiety. When the seventh seal was opened, heaven became silent. This is what the knight discovers. God is silent. People dwell in fearful isolation. Only death speaks. The knight arrives at his castle and finds everyone waiting to die. It is a loveless reunion. The final scene is viewed through the eyes of the juggler, as he watches the knight and his family, led by the grim reaper in a dance of death along the bare cliffs by the sea.

The story could fit John's time and, in many ways, our own. There is an apocalyptic mood today, especially as the year 2000 approaches. The seventh seal has been opened for many and God is silent. Some even say God is dead. Environmentalists march with costumes decorated with skulls and lament the death of the water and the danger in the violet-rayed skies. Political instability is widespread. The church struggles to maintain the virtues of Christianity — embedded in the Sermon on the Mount — in the face of a culture that crazily preaches the exact opposite. Death camps, wars, famines, AIDS, and doomsday weapons comprise the modern version of the Black Plague.

In Bergman's film, the director makes us look at the juggler's family, whose lightness of heart sustains the faith and common sense denied by the extremism of everyone else. Here is the jester who celebrates life and affirms it against the universal agony. The film director searches for hints of hope during this time of the silence of heaven.

Beautiful as this is, it is a pale effort. The church has much richer resources for hope for the human spirit. The church has the boundless energies of grace, available through prayer and the power of the Spirit. The grandeur of the Book of Revelation reveals the pulsing reality of heaven pushing against the stubborn resistance of earth. The stirring force of Love, bursting from the victorious Lamb, wants to make life erupt in our consciousness and in our world.

The corruption of our culture spends too much time with the decay of death and attempts to legalize it in abortion and euthanasia. But Jesus is greater than this. His love is stronger than death. The culture tries to make death seem sweet. Jesus will have none of this. Death is sour and should be overcome by the sturdy sweetness of eternal life, experienced already here in the sacraments and possessed absolutely in heaven.

What gifts for our souls do we find in chapter seven? What shall we do with these gifts?

1. *Hope. Pit Christian hope against fashionable despair.* Modern culture spends too much time and money on things and on seeing how the human body is connected to the animal world. This is a self-defeating strategy. It is a sure recipe for despair. We can love things, but things cannot love us. It is like talking to a wall; the wall cannot talk back. At best it can only give us an echo of ourselves. Loneliness is the result.

Think of all the research devoted to solving human problems by seeing how animals act. Why are we so aggressive? Well look at how predatory animals are. We have, so they say, inherited that from our animal ancestors. There may be some truth in evolution, but am I really headed for self improvement by looking at my link with apes?

Christianity directly opposes both positions. It teaches that happiness is a spiritual affair, not a material one. Joy comes from loving persons, both human and divine. Things are meant to serve the purposes of loving relationships, not to be ends in themselves. The church also teaches that we should concentrate on the connection between our souls and God, not on our similarity to the animals. Adam named the animals. He did not try to identify with them or seek solutions to his loneliness problem with them. Only God and another human being could do that. Hence God provided him with Eve.

Hope is essentially a spiritual matter. There is no hope in things, only in love. There is no hope in looking backward to the animal world, only in a forward look to the surge of our souls to their heavenly destiny. We should pit Christian hope against the fashionable despair of our day.

Hope is a Christian gift. John stirred up hope in the persecuted church of his day. We should explode with hope as our gift to a culture wallowing in too much death and despair. Tell them, as did John to the seven churches, "God will wipe away every tear from their eyes" (7:17).

2. *Confidence. Practice Christian expansiveness.* Over two thousand years, Christianity has been the source of titanic energies for magnificent civilizations. Famous opinion makers today preach "decline," decline of western culture, of western ideals, of western ability to achieve. There may be some truth to this. Only good people can be a great people. Only those who believe in the importance of virtue, responsibility, and accountability can produce a vibrant culture.

When people give in to their lower appetites and choose evil over good, then the culture declines. Culture needs the driving force of love, morality, and self-discipline. Evil restricts life and growth. Virtue (comes from a Latin word meaning power and strength) expands life and development.

If people cease to have character they lose their self-confidence. Self-worth is not improved by superficial flattery. A hug and a compliment are like an aspirin, helpful yes, but not effective for the moral combat that really gives a person confidence. Self-worth only grows in the hard fought battle to acquire moral and spiritual character. The church has never forgotten the dynamic gift of confidence that makes civilization possible. The formula is ageless. Lose the self. Take the cross. Follow Jesus. This is the secret of confidence and the acquisition of self-worth. Culture shrinks when it is missing. Culture expands gloriously when it is present. John poured confidence into his first Christians. His message will do the same for us today.

Reflection

1. How would I best explain the meaning of the number of 144,000 of the elect?
2. Why does John give us a picture of the final victory of the elect? How does it help me personally?
3. Since Vatican II, the number of non-Christians has doubled. What does that mean for our missionary efforts?
4. In what ways do I share my faith with others?
5. Before the opening of the seventh seal, there is a half hour of silence in heaven. How do I react to the silence of God?
6. What impression does the story of Bergman's Seventh Seal make on me? What similarities do I see today?
7. What stories of lack of hope could I tell from my own experience?
8. How do I build up the Spirit's gift of hope in my life?
9. What examples of loss of confidence do I see in our culture?
10. What do I do to increase my confidence in self, others, God?

Prayer

Risen Lord, you have already won the victory over sin's ability to enslave us. Even now heaven is peopled with countless numbers of those who have won, through you, the victory over sin on earth and now enjoy the absolute human and spiritual fulfillment you promised. The triumph of the elect inspires us on our pilgrimage. I know that only a good people become a great culture. Renew in me the gifts of hope and confidence that I may bring these virtues to our culture.

8 Hell Is in Session

The Resurgence of Belief in Hell

Hell is every believer's worst nightmare. The prospect of punishment for the intransigent wicked beyond the grave has been part of Christian teaching since the time of Jesus. St. Jerome visualized it as a hot, fiery state of sensory punishment. Origen thought it was a place only of spiritual suffering. Augustine said it was both a bodily and spiritual torment. The early church fathers held that hell was a punishment. Origen argued it was medicinal, that in hell the worst sinners could be reclaimed for God. The bishops at the Council of Constantinople in A.D. 543 rejected this. Later, some theologians proposed that hell eventually annihilated the souls. The church rejected this as well. Hell is everlasting.

For much of the twentieth century, hell has been ignored. Hell disappeared and no one noticed. The intellectuals dismissed it. It seemed as nothing when compared to Hiroshima and the Holocaust. Priests and ministers stopped preaching about it in most cases. One veteran preacher testified he had not preached about hell in thirty years.

But hell is making a comeback. Seventy-two percent of Americans say they believe in hell. Young and old alike are in this group. Mainline Protestants, Catholics, and Evangelicals all agree. When asked if they were likely to go to hell, most of them said no. This is a "cake and eat it too" approach to unpleasant outcomes of unrepented sinful behavior. Many like to say there is a hell, but no one is there. This is a long way from Teresa of Avila who had a vision in which she saw souls falling into hell like leaves from an autumn tree.

The revival of belief in hell is part of a broader religious renewal and a return to traditional religion. The violence in our streets and the pervasive suffering that has resulted from alcoholism, drugs, AIDS, and other afflictions makes belief in hell more accessible.

Jesus was forthright about hell. He called it "gehenna," a place of everlasting fire, reserved for those who refuse to believe and be converted. All who cause others to sin and all evildoers will be thrown "into the fiery furnace where there will be wailing and grinding of teeth" (Mt. 13:42). This punishment will last forever. "Depart from me, you accursed, into the eternal fire prepared for the devil and his angels" (Mt. 25:41). Following the example of Christ, the church has warned the faithful in every age of the sad and lamentable reality of eternal death, also called hell.

The First Four Trumpets (8:6-13)

The above reflection on hell fits very well into our meditation on the Seven Trumpets in the Book of Revelation. Each blast of the trumpet signals another woe for the wicked. The judgment is always a two-sided affair, salvation for the faithful and damnation for the evil ones. Revelation establishes this teaching with three sets of seven plagues as dramatized in the Seven Seals, the Seven Trumpets, and the Seven Bowls of Wrath (cf. chapter 16).

It is easy to see the repetitiveness in these three sets of woes. There is always an audience in the heavenly throne room, a vision of the elect and music of praise for the gift of salvation. Then follows a series of afflictions, mainly directed to those who hope to destroy the church. Biblical writers would not consider this mere repetition. Scriptural minds think in cycles and spirals. We tend to think in a line, a logical progression from point one to point two to the conclusion. Along the way we add facts, details, and evidence to support the argument.

On the other hand, biblical thinking is cyclical and like a spiral. Some comparisons may help. Think of a single violin playing a melody such as the "Star Spangled Banner." Then hear it again played by the London symphony orchestra. Finally, hear it once more with the violin, the symphony, and now with the Mormon Tabernacle choir. It is still the original melody, but what a difference in richness and emotional impact upon our hearts.

Or visualize a great Shakespearean actor such as Laurence Olivier. Watch him alone on a stage reciting "To be or not to be," from *Hamlet*. It is a rehearsal and he is wearing a turtleneck and jeans. Next, see him suited up in Hamlet's costume giving a solo performance of various readings from the bard. Finally, enjoy him dramatically delivering his lines in a full-blown production at Stratford, England. It is the same soliloquy in each case, only the spiral has lifted it to texture and meaning beyond a simple recitation.

In Revelation a principal theme is the judgment against sinners. John presents this truth in ever mounting richness — a spiral. First he lays out the experiences that flowed from the opening of the seals. When he finishes — with that perfect seven — it seems as though everything has been said.

But then he comes back and roams over the same observations in his vision of the Seven Trumpets. He raises the listeners awareness to new levels. There is mind expansion from the original woes to a catastrophe much more lasting than imagined in the first set. The wicked are not just going to suffer. They will agonize forever. John is talking about hell, the ultimate judgment against the unrepentant sinner.

The Seven Trumpets would seem to close off any further descriptions. Yet John will return again to the plagues and woes in his review of the Seven Bowls of Wrath. The spiral of judgment had risen from the seals to the trumpets. Now the spiral surges upward in the bowls of wrath and conveys the intensity of God's opposition to evil in a manner that would not be felt so deeply without the previous steps in the process.

Let us now listen to the sound of the Seven Trumpets and hear what they reveal.

Environmental Disaster (First Trumpet). Hail and fire mixed with blood ravage the forests and meadows incinerating all vegetation. The green is gone.

Notice three things as we go through this list of woes. First, the tribulations sound very similar to the ten plagues that God sent against Pharaoh in the Old Testament. Secondly, the process is the reverse of creation. The seven days of creation are replaced with the seven moments of de-creation. Thirdly, not all of creation is affected, only one third of it. Hence this is not yet the whole story of the judgement.

A Sea of Blood (Second Trumpet). A burning mountain spews itself into the sea and turns it blood-red. It kills fish and destroys ships. John may have borrowed this image from a volcano, possibly Vesuvius, whose explosion and lava flow would produce just what he is describing. It reminds us of the first plague in Egypt. And he "changed into blood their streams — their running water, so that they could not drink" (Ps. 78:44).

A Falling Star (Third Trumpet). A large star, burning like a torch, fell from the sky. It turned drinking water sour as though affected by wormwood, a desert plant that had a bitter taste. The Old Testament linked wormwood with the bitterness of God's judgment against those who were unfaithful, the idolatrous for example. Jeremiah said as much to the people of his time who abandoned God and worshiped the Baals (false gods). "See now, I will give them wormwood to eat and poison to drink" (Jer. 9:14).

Darkness at Noon (Fourth Trumpet). One third of the sky suffers a blackout. We are reminded of a similar event in the story of Moses in Egypt. God tells him, "Stretch out your hand toward the sky, that over the land of Egypt there may be such intense darkness that one can feel it" (Ex. 10:21).

Before John hears the fifth trumpet he sees an eagle rushing through the sky and announcing the coming of the next three tribulations. When God wants to comfort us with hope, he sends a dove of peace to hover quietly in the sky. When God discloses the punishment that is caused by our self-destructive sinfulness, he sends the warlike eagle to soar above the earth with this calamitous message.

Reflection

1. When was the last time I heard a sermon on hell? What did I think of it?
2. How does my belief in hell affect my moral behavior?
3. If the love of God alone should keep me from sinning, then why use fear of hell as a motivation for good behavior?
4. John's vision of the seals, the trumpets, and the bowls of wrath

repeat the same messages. It is spiral thinking. What does that mean?

5. What does the sound of trumpets do to me?
6. Trumpet sounds can signal joy and also sorrow, such as "taps" at a military funeral. What are examples of trumpet sounds referring to disasters?
7. In our "feel-good" society why is it so hard to think of God's judgments against sin and evil?
8. Why do we need the blast of a trumpet as a wake-up call to avoid sin and evil?
9. What are some "signs of the times" that are contemporary "trumpets" calling us to conversion and spiritual renewal?
10. In the midst of the noisy trumpets, God puts a peaceful dove in the sky. Why does God give us this symbol of hope and forgiveness?

Prayer

Lord of judgment, you love me so much that you want to wake me from my spiritual and moral apathy. You desire my eternal happiness and want to fill me with love. Sometimes you need to reach me with the startling sound of a trumpet — an event that moves me to hear your voice and return to you. I praise you and bless you for this compassionate gift.

9 A Closer Look

Opening the Gates of Hell (9:1-12)

Up to this point the afflictions of sinners have been natural catastrophes. Sinners have broken the natural law and it has revolted against them with hail, fire, burnt forests, a devastated sea, a ruined water supply, and a dark smog worse than any so far known. The next punishments are unnatural, or preternatural — beyond the natural order. The force of hell is unleashed upon the earth.

The fifth trumpet sounds. A power comet falls from the sky, plunges to the earth with a force that opens up the very gates of hell. "It opened the passage to . . . the abyss" (verse 2). Biblical imagination thought of hell as a world underneath the earth. Actually, there were two such worlds.

One was *Sheol*, the abode of the dead who had died reconciled to God. It was a "waiting room" where the souls of the just were housed until redemption. In our Creed we say that after his death, Jesus descended into hell. This was not the hell of the damned, but the resting place of the just. In Christian thinking Jesus met all the souls of history who had remained faithful to God. Jesus brought them the Good News of their imminent resurrection with him and their forthcoming passage to heaven.

The second room in the underworld was the hell of the damned. This is the place that was prepared for the devil and his angels. We should make it clear here that we are dealing with mysterious realities. Biblical imagination dealt with them in pictorial and concrete terms — two rooms (Sheol and Hell) underneath the crust of the earth. It is not good geology by our modern, scientific standards, but it is correct theology. Maybe they were naive about their cosmogony, but they were adult about their theology. We tend to be adult about our cosmogony and childish in our theology.

Hell is not a physical place in our sense of the term. Neither is heaven for that matter. Nonetheless, our faith tells us that it is real. Our souls are not physical, but they are real. Because we can experience our souls here, we sense our own personal mystery. We are urged to live "spiritual lives" as well as physical ones. We use exercise and diet to take care of our bodies. We use prayer and meditation and sacraments and virtuous living to take care of our souls.

Millions of people of faith have told us that in the aging process, the body declines and fades, but the soul grows stronger and becomes more self evident to us. The more we become aware of our souls, the more we understand they are not confined by the physical. In some strange way our souls are associated with our present bodies, but not absolutely tied to a place.

So it is with hell and heaven. We no longer look above the sky for heaven or underneath the earth for hell. We appreciate that the existence of heaven and hell — like our souls — belongs to a non-physical "world" that is more real and lasting than the physical one. This should not permit us to feel superior to our biblical cousins who relied on physical images to grasp spiritual realities.

This much must be said for them, they had no doubts about the reality of heaven and hell. And for us, alas, it should be said that our scientific sophistication has often weakened our appreciation of spiritual realities. I am not arguing for a return to blunt physical comparisons that have no scientific value. I am saying that we should discover a language for spiritual realities suitable to our own day.

Mutant Locusts

The punishment of the wicked that comes from hell is so fierce that it can only be called demonic. John uses images that even our science fiction horror thrillers have scarcely matched. Unearthly terrors harm the evil ones. The abyss of hell opens and evil people feel the hot blast and smoke of a gigantic furnace. A plague of locusts approaches sinners.

In modern genetic terms these locusts are not just big grasshoppers, they are mutants. They are monsters the size of horses trained for war. They have human faces and abundant hair. Their teeth are as big and sharp as a lion's and their chests like iron breastplates. When their wings flap they make sounds like a hurricane wind.

They have scorpion tails that sting with fatal and painful poison. Instead of instantly killing their victims, the scorpion poison suspends them in unbearable pain for five months. A scorpion is like a small lobster with claws to clutch its prey. It has a long tail which curves over its back and over its head. At the end of the tail is a curved claw. With this claw the scorpion strikes the victim and secretes its poison.

"They had as their king the angel of the abyss, whose name in Hebrew is Abaddon and in Greek Apollyon" (verse 11). Abaddon means death and destruction. Apollyon means the destroyer.

Here again we are dealing with similes, metaphors, comparisons. Biblical people knew this just as we do. They realized they were trying to speak about mysterious realities, in this case the awesome outcome of a life of unrepentant sinning. They did not sanitize the truth and make it look smooth and irrelevant. They did not allow a standard of tastefulness to hide the eternal pain that an unregenerate sinner would suffer. True, it may not be caused by a mutant locust with a scorpion's tail. Sinners make their own bed of alienation from God, others, and self. Sin is self-destructive. The image of the punishing monster was a dramatic device to make this truth plain.

Today we put all these monsters into science-fiction horror films or Stephen King terror novels for entertainment purposes. We pay hundreds of millions of dollars to feel the shivers. We do not use these symbols to remind us of the pains of the damned. This is all right. What is not all right is our denial of hell and the potential eternal suffering we would experience should we die estranged from God.

Hell's Blitzkrieg (9:13-21)

The sixth trumpet sounds and announces the coming of hell's army to kill the wicked. Four avenging angels ride forth on horses, colored fiery red, smoky blue, and sulphurous yellow. In other words, the four horsemen of the vision of the seven seals are back. Remember what I said earlier about cyclical and spiral thinking. Here is repetition but at another level. The first time the punishment was natural and earthly. Now it is unnatural and hellish.

The mutant locusts cause lasting pain. The sulphurous horses cause lasting death, not a death without pain, but a death of loveless loneliness, a death of existence with no meaning. The tails of the horses are like snakes' heads inflicting death on sinners. A third of the world's people die. One would think that this would cause repentance and conversion in those who survived.

Without a doubt these signs of judgment do cause spiritual renewal in those who can read the signs of the times. Prayer and penance are taken up by many. Sadly, many others fail to get the point. "The rest of the human race, who were not killed by these plagues, did not repent. . . . Nor did they repent of their murders, their magic potions, their unchastity, or their robberies" (verse 20). Sin blinds the sinner, hardens the heart, and stiffens the neck. Sin captures the psychology of the person and enslaves the soul. The grace of conversion, implored by the prayers and penances of the just, is paramount for the salvation of sinners.

Where do we go with this kind of meditation? What are the results for our personal lives? What shall we do?

Prepare for Your Ultimate Future — Life After Death

When we are young we dream about the future. Naturally, this is a future in this present world. Our youthful ideals, helped along by surging vitality and natural energy, make us think of success, happiness, and the world's recognition of our talents. When we pass our mid-life crisis and head for old age, we settle for less. We take life's setbacks, disappointments, and trials more in stride.

We muse about the days of our youth and the ideals that were never fulfilled as we hoped. We did not foresee the roadblocks in our rosy future planning. Now we return to dreams about the future, only this time we gaze across that mysterious boundary that separates us from life beyond the grave. What awaits us after death? What kind of a future will we have?

We know we will all die. Our faith tells us that our souls will survive physical death. Christ's resurrection assures us that one day our bodies will rise and in some mysterious way be rejoined to our souls. We have no scientific way of verifying any of this. Only faith can be our guide. If we hope to have the eternal joy of heaven in the next life, we must plan for it here. Everything depends on the choices we make here. Either we choose Jesus, his person, message, and grace, or we do not. All our lives are a record of the choices we have made. I am what I have chosen.

When I choose sin, I also opt for unlove. I walk a path that encumbers the outcome of sin — pain, loss, death. As long as I live on this earth, I am free to change from sin to love, from evil to grace, from selfishness to Jesus. But after death I cannot change my mind any more. My last breath concludes all choosing. If I die refusing God's love, then that is how I will exist after death. If I die welcoming God's love, that divine affection will flood my heart forever.

"It is appointed that human beings die once, and after this the judgment" (Heb. 9:27). God's judgment does not differ from the judgment we made for our own lives. His judgment comes as no surprise, for our choices have led us to where we wanted to be. In this life there are judgment signs — pain, war, disease, betrayal, famine, earthquakes, hurricanes, murder, theft, and so on. Some we bring on ourselves. Others are part of the general sinfulness. The experience of judgment in this life is a sign of the times meant to call us to repentance and conversion. That is the very point of the colorful and awesome judgment scenes in the Book of Revelation. But after death the judgment is final, one way or the other, hell or heaven. Today is the day to make the right choice, to plan for the only future really worth having.

Reflection

1. What impact does John's description of the mutant locusts from hell have on me?
2. How have experiences of natural disasters or personal tragedies affected my moral and spiritual life?

3. Today's horror films make lots of money. Why are they so popular? How do they differ from the horrors described in Revelation?
4. How am I planning for my future in the afterlife?
5. I become what I choose. I am the sum of my choices. What does that mean?
6. If I could change my mind after I die, what would that mean for my life before I died?
7. Surveys tell us that most people believe in hell, but few of them believe they will ever go there. What do I think of this?
8. If asked, how would I describe hell?
9. Some say we should only use love of God and never fear of hell to motivate people to avoid evil. What is my view?
10. The "now generation" and the "me people" hate to think of death and the afterlife. How could I help them overcome this massive denial?

Prayer

Jesus, my judge, you will confirm after my death the way I lived in this life. Awaken my conscience today so that I make the choices that lead me to choose you and love. Make me aware of the necessity of planning for life after death. Jolt me from complacency by the signs of my times, the experiences of judgment you give me before I die. Thank you for such gifts and graces. I want to change now before it is too late.

10 Get Ready for Joy

Like a good psychologist, John does not overplay his hand. Having stunned and, perhaps, scared us with his unremitting picture of hell, he pulls back from the flow of the judgment visions. Chapters 10 and 11 are time-out's from the noise and clangor of the divine war against the wicked. John turns his attention tenderly to the little flock who has remained faithful to Jesus.

He introduces the theme of joy which the elect will experience haltingly on earth, splendidly in heaven. Drawing back from the jaws of hell, John gives hints of the comforts of heaven. The message was "like sweet honey" in his mouth (10:10). A joyful outcome awaits the "servants, the prophets and the holy ones" (11:18).

Spiritual Joy

We should preface our meditation on these chapters with some thoughts about the nature of spiritual joy. Philosopher Peter Kreeft gives us a useful model for getting at this experience. Imagine you stand at the edge of a canyon. Plant a sign that says "body." Underneath it write, "Pleasure satisfies the body." Now hike down to the middle of the canyon. Post a second sign that says "mind." Beneath it write, "Happiness satisfies the mind." Finally, make your way to the bottom of the canyon. Erect a sign that says "spirit." On it write, "Joy satisfies the soul." This picture is an image of our inner life and its three kinds of satisfaction.

Taste chocolate and feel the sensation of *pleasure.* Acquire knowledge and solve problems and experience *happiness.* Lastly, meet the Holy Spirit deep within your heart and know what *joy* is like. Bodily pleasure does not last. It requires new stimulation, be that sexual, or a high from running, or an affectionate hug. Mind happiness does not last. Our restless minds keep looking for new worlds to conquer, more knowledge to acquire, fresh problems to solve. The only thing that really lasts is joy — the love we experience in an encounter with the Holy Spirit of Jesus. Time after time saints tell us that they have received the gift of joy even in the midst of bodily pain or soul torments.

It is true that for most of us, even joy seems temporary. That is because we draw back from our relationship with the Spirit and settle for less — bodily pleasure and mental happiness. Now I realize I am using the term joy in a special sense, namely, the satisfaction from union with the Spirit. Joy feels a bit like pleasure and happiness, but its source is eternal and its impact is qualitatively different. Joy in the Spirit makes us realize that there is an eternal experience available to us. It is, as the Irish say, a little bit of heaven here on earth.

Pleasure gives us excitement without peace because we keep grubbing for more sensations, crying for madder music and stronger wine. Happiness gives us the opposite, peace without excitement. The forces of our minds and the moral self-control that results makes us feel mastery. What is lacking, however, is passion, excitement. But when we have union with the Spirit, we have both excitement and peace simultaneously. We have a passion for God and a peace beyond all understanding.

This works because nothing comes from ourselves. We have not taken a drug to excite us and give us peace. We have not made ourselves into great moral examples through discipline and thus are at peace but in a loveless, unexciting kind of way. (This does not mean we should abandon self-mastery, but rather incorporate it into the third stage.) The reason why we can have peace and passion in the third step is because we are totally surrendered to the best source of each — the Spirit of ecstasy (passion) and peace.

This is why the saints tell us about ecstasy. They are not talking about some dreamy state that withdraws them from this world. The term ecstasy here does not refer to a frantic trance into which we project ourselves, such as happens in a whirling dance. Ecstasy is being drawn away from the control of our lives by ourselves and entrusting them to God. The word ecstasy (*ek-stasis* in Greek) means to stand outside ourselves. Hence in spiritual joy we are not "in" love, so much as love is in us. Divine love — the divine Lover — is the moving force of our lives.

This brief reflection about the nature of heavenly joy in that part of our inner life where we meet the Holy Spirit offers us the proper mood to approach the interlude which John gives us in chapters 10 and 11. For a moment he has come back to earth and reaches out with sympathy to the nervous little Christian communities. Jesus has given him this mission as we will now see.

The Honey-Coated Scroll (10:1-11)

The heavenly scene temporarily vanishes. John is momentarily back on earth amid the familiar sights of Patmos. He sees a big angel who places one foot on the land and his other foot on the sea. This giant heavenly messenger speaks so loud it sounds like the roar of a lion or repeated claps of thunder. The angel reads from a small scroll. When he finished, he raised his right hand to the sky and swore that this was God's truth. His closing statement indicated that the faithful should be encouraged because God's actions against their persecutors would soon take place. "There shall be no more delay" (verse 6).

Dutifully, John takes up his pen and begins to write down this most recent message. But the angel orders him not to communicate this revelation. There are some secrets shared by God that are only for the visionary and no one else. St. Paul wrote of a similar experience. "This person was caught up into Paradise and heard ineffable things which no man may utter" (II Cor. 12:4). Catholics, familiar with the visions of Our Lady of Fatima, have long speculated about the "secret" of Fatima, a revelation to Sister Lucy not meant for publication except to the pope. God sometimes communicates a special secret to a loved one, a message that may well be beyond both the understanding of the receiver or people at large.

The revelation of the secret will come in due time when history is ready. Scripture is full of the noiseless course of God's providential work. The prophet Malachi had predicted that one day the Lord would suddenly come to his temple (Mal. 3:1). Centuries passed and even students of the Bible had forgotten about it. Then, abruptly, Jesus was born and brought by Joseph and his Blessed Mother to be presented to God at the temple.

It is a simple and ordinary scene. This poor couple brings the humble offerings of doves. An old man, Simeon, takes the child in his arms and praises God. An old woman, Anna, thanks God for this baby. Nothing impressive. No shouts for attention to Jesus. The world would see them simply as another of thousands of humble Jewish parents doing their duty.

But in their arms was the Savior of the world, disguised as a stranger in his own house. Yet the glory of God quietly shone in the temple. And this through the humble gathering of a baby, his parents, and two senior citizens. The pilgrims that day noticed nothing, but St. Luke preserved the scene for us and every February 2nd the universal church lights candles and sings hymns at the liturgy that celebrates this coming of glory to the temple.

The world is always blind and profane. It does not see divine warnings in the upheavals of nature and history. It searches out rational explanations of cosmic and political troubles. So there is an aspect of God's revelation that becomes secret. God seems to hide his providence, yet always carry it forward. Jesus appeared briefly again in the temple when he was twelve. Just that one extra time in thirty years. Between the first and the final self-revelation of Jesus in the temple, a whole generation of people died off. They missed the glory and its meaning for their lives.

When the angel told John to seal the newest message in a secret file, he was teaching this truth about the secret action of divine providence in history, but one that will suddenly appear when the time was right.

The angel then told John to swallow the scroll. He found that it tasted sweet, like honey in his mouth. But when it went to his stomach it left him with a sour taste. This refers to the "sweet and sour" nature of the prophetic vocation. When he preaches God's word to the willing listeners and believers, that is a sweet experience. When he shares God's word with hostile and unwilling hearers, that is a bitter moment, especially when they reject God and make the prophet suffer for his message.

Reflection

1. Why are bodily pleasures and mental happinesses temporary?
2. Why would spiritual joy be experienced as lasting?
3. What motivates John to take time to console his little flock?
4. God gives John a mystical "secret" to keep. Mary gave Sister Lucy a secret at Fatima. What do I think of such secrets?
5. The scroll tasted like honey in John's mouth, but was sour in his stomach. How does this experience apply to his ministry?
6. Years ago, fire and brimstone sermons were popular. Today, joy and love homilies are preferred. What might I consider a more realistic and balanced approach?
7. Follow Peter Kreeft's "canyon steps" at the beginning of this chapter. Why does his guidance make so much sense?
8. What are some experiences in my life that I would call ecstatic? What was so ecstatic about them?
9. What kind of "bursts of joy" would I like to have in the future?
10. Religion without joy is a burden. Religion without sorrow is unreal. What then should I expect from religion?

Prayer

God of my joy, I exult in the revelation of your loving presence. I thank you for the happiness you grant me. At the same time I know I must continue on the road of the cross and the loss of my selfishness. Still, it is your joy-filled strength that makes my path to the cross possible and the Easter fulfillment, its spiritual outcome, a trusted truth. Thank you, Lord.

11 The Spiritual Power of Christian Witness

The Witnessing Church (11:1-14)

Witnesses who practice the Gospel are always more convincing than preachers who talk a lot but do not witness their words. People trust more in witnesses than in mere speakers. Experience moves people more than theories do. Jesus was an outstanding witness of his own message.

The first form of Christian witness is the life of the Christian. Another powerful witness is the Church when as a loving and faithful community she exhibits what the teachings of Jesus are all about. When, despite all human limitations and weaknesses, a Christian displays a simplicity of life after the example of Jesus, that person is a sign of the presence of God and heavenly reality.

The kind of Christian witness that has the most appeal for the world is concern for people, love for the poor and the weak and those in pain. The attractive generosity that energizes this behavior is in absolute contrast to selfishness. When Christians commit themselves to the quest for peace, the defense of human rights, and the proper development of the human person, then the world is able to see how the Gospel works in practice.

God has called the church to bear witness to Jesus by taking courageous stands against political and economic corruption. The Church must never seek her own glory or material wealth. What resources she has should be devoted to the poorest of the poor and the imitation of Christ's own simplicity of life.

Keep this view of a witnessing church in mind as you read chapter 11 of Revelation. John received a command to measure the temple and count those who worship there. He was not to measure the court of the gentiles. In other words, John was asked to evaluate the church of his day and estimate how strong was its witness in that time of trouble.

He finds that the church, as a community, was a living witness to Christ. Yes, in his letters to the seven churches, he found deficiencies, but overall the church was living up to its calling as is evident here. He uses the example of "two witnesses" to show how effectively the church was making Jesus known. He borrowed this image from the two great witnesses of the Old Testament, Moses, and Elijah. They represented the essence of Jewish religion, the law and the prophets. The law encompassed the covenant union with God and how to fulfill that love. The prophets, being the conscience of Israel, brought the people back to the purity of covenant observance.

Both Moses and Elijah were prophetic, that is, witnesses of Jewish covenant observance. They personalized Jewish religious witness. The word prophet implies witness. John calls them two olive trees. Such trees symbolized life and immortality. Their witness endures. He also called them two lampstands. They personalized the church. The Christian church shows the same kind of durability and power.

They close up the sky so that no rain comes when they prophesy. Elijah had done that when he prophesied against the evil kings of his day. The rainless sky was a sign of judgment against sin. They bring the plagues. Moses had done so in Egypt. Again a sign of judgment against those who afflict God's people. The church of John's day would carry his Revelation message about the coming judgment against Rome.

Why does John pick Old Testament heroes to symbolize the new church? Probably because the church is so new and its outstanding heroes are not yet fixed in Christian consciousness the way such "giants of old" are in the memory at least of Jewish Christians. Moses and Elijah are, without question, heroes of faith. It is true he does not actually name them in this passage, but the references to closing up the sky and sending plagues obviously refers to them.

The witnessing church will face fatal opposition. "The beast that comes up from the abyss will wage war against them and conquer them and kill them" (verse 7). Who is the beast? Ultimately it is Satan who rules the abyss, a name for hell. The beast is also the "Antichrist" who will figure prominently in the chapters to come. We will see him again as the Dragon and as beast in chapter 13. I will reserve my comments about the role of the Anti-Christ for chapter 13.

The beast will leave the church like a corpse in the street of the great city. John gives the city symbolic names such as Sodom and Egypt to indicate how evil it is. The citizens compound the humiliation by demanding that the corpses of Christian witnesses be denied burial for three and one half days so that the victors can gloat over their triumph. But like Jesus, the witnessing church will rise from the dead. "After the three and a half days, the breath of life from God entered them. When they stood on their feet, great fear fell on those who saw them" (verse 11). They watched in astonishment as a voice from heaven called the martyrs to heavenly glory. The ultimate form of witnessing is to die for Christ. The ultimate reward is resurrection to new life in Christ.

Songs of Thankfulness and Praise (11:13-19)

This chapter closes with another glimpse of the joy of heaven. The seventh trumpet sounds. The martyrs of the witnessing church are now before the throne of God joining in the music of praise. The words of the hymn glorify God for being stronger than the power groups on earth. Hymns such as this one would also be sung in the house churches all across the empire. These hymns both celebrated the power of the witnessing church, the victory of the martyrs, and served as a music of hope for those who still remained to fight the spiritual battles. As they locked arms, supporting one another, they thanked God. "To recompense your servants, the prophets, and the holy ones and those who fear your name, the small and the great alike" (verse 18).

A final detail. As the temple of heaven opened, John could see the Ark of the Covenant. The old ark had contained the tablets of the ten commandments and remnants of the manna. It stood for the absolute love God had for his people and the union between them.

The earthly ark was lost in the sands of time. The heavenly ark remains now as a Christian symbol of a permanent covenant made by Christ.

How do we become Christian witnesses today?

1. *Trust in the power of silent witness.* We must show that we are able to understand and accept others. We should be ready to cooperate with all people of good will to make a better community and a more loving world. It ought to be clear that our pursuit of virtue for the common good is derived from attitudes that are traceable to a divine origin. Our Christian goodness should be such that it raises questions about the reasons for our behavior. Why are they like this? Why do they live this way? Why do they reach out to us with such affection? This is a strong, silent witness, a proclamation of the Gospel in action.

This kind of witness will touch many classes of people. It will affect those who are immersed in the secular culture of our society and who have no connection with the church. It will exert a positive influence on the millions of our fellow baptized who have fallen away from active membership in the church. It will excite the searchers for truth and meaning. They look for God but need to encounter someone who is deeply committed to Christ and who shows it in loving concern for others. This means we will need to be actively present to these various peoples in our society. If they never meet us they are not likely to be touched.

2. *Silent witness is not enough. Use word witness too.* Silent witness captures people's attention and affects their hearts. But this is not enough. We must also be ready to share our faith. The faith needs explanation. We need to explain the source of our activity. Jesus was the greatest witness to salvation and the kingdom who ever lived. At the same time he verbally proclaimed these spiritual realities and explained what they meant for daily life. Jesus showed us how to share the Word of God. St. Peter says, "Always be ready to give an explanation to anyone who asks you for a reason for your hope" (I Pt. 3:15).

The Gospel proclaimed by the silent witness of loving behavior must be complemented by the public witness of the Word of God. At some point, we have to tell people about Jesus, who he is and what he said and did. Beyond this we also must invite others to accept in faith the person and message of Jesus, membership in the church, active participation in the sacraments, and a moral life based on the Gospel. We do more than share information. We are — by the power of the Spirit — converters of persons to Christ and the church.

Intellectual acceptance is insufficient. We share a Christian way of life. Christianity was originally called, "The Way." We introduce a three step process: (1) Information about Jesus; (2) Formation in Christian life; (3) Transformation of the person by the grace of the Holy Spirit. This is the full Gospel action. Its final result is a new Christian who in turn becomes a silent witness and a public Word witness to others.

This is often challenging and difficult. Chapter 11 of Revelation shows how bloody the difficulty becomes in some cases, as in those of the martyrs. But nothing worthwhile in life happens without challenge. There is no crown without a cross. This has happened millions of times in the church's two-thousand-year-old history. It can and will happen again today.

Do you want to be part of it?

Reflection

1. How would I interpret John's use of Moses and Elijah as examples of the faithful witness of the church?
2. What are ways whereby I witness the teachings of Jesus in my personal behavior?
3. Why should I be willing to witness the virtues of Jesus in my community?
4. Why is it insufficient to witness silently? Why is sharing my faith with others important?
5. Sharing information about Jesus is one step. What is the argument in favor of inviting others to commit themselves to Jesus and the church?
6. Why am I more impressed with someone who practices what he says than someone who doesn't?
7. What areas of Christian witness touch me most today?
8. Why does persecution make stronger Christians?

9. How do I feel about the Christians of Eastern Europe who withstood Communist oppression?
10. Some say our secular culture is undermining our faith. How would I witness Christ in the face of this?

Prayer

Jesus, you are the cause of my joy. Because of your willingness to share your joy with me, I begin to know even here on earth what eternal joy is like. The result is that I am privileged to be simultaneously filled with peace and also the excitement of being a living witness of the Gospel. I praise you and thank you for establishing your rule in my heart.

12 A Woman's Pain — A Dragon's Defeat

The Pain of the Woman

Nothing creative happens without pain. The greatest artists anguish to produce the best creations. Mothers suffer to create their babies and nourish them into adulthood. Not everyone can create a public work of art. But each person can produce an internal art work, a moral character. With the help of the Spirit, each of us can shape the interior masterpiece — our personal art work. None of us can do it without pain.

Mary, the mother of Jesus, became one of the world's greatest art works through her blessed Son. Pain marked each passage in this process. When she presented him in the temple, she heard Simeon predict that the heart of her motherhood would be pierced by a sword. To protect Jesus, she went into exile in Egypt. When he was twelve, she experienced the panic of temporarily losing Jesus. On Good Friday, she met him on the way to Calvary, saw him nailed to the cross, experienced his death, held his dead body in her arms, and buried him in the grave.

Yet the pain of Mary was not a useless passion. It was a birth pang. The pain that began at Bethlehem became the joy of Easter and the ecstasy of Pentecost. The secular world believes it has a human right not to suffer. The woman of faith understood that pain is the price of creativity. Of course it was not easy. It was a battle, a moral warfare. But by the power of God, the ultimate source of creativity, Jesus was born, the church was born, Christians are born.

The Story Behind the Story

This is the splendid message of this next vision of St. John. In chapters 12-14, we come to the core of the Book of Revelation. We hear the story behind the story of what went before and what lies ahead. If we missed the point behind the messages of the Seven Seals and the Seven Trumpets, we will have no excuse after we contemplate the Woman and the Dragon, the Lamb and the Beast.

In these passages, John raises his "picture theology" to an art form. So much grandeur flows from his palette that some compare his masterpiece to the Sistine Chapel. There Michelangelo sweeps us back to creation and forward to the last judgment. John does the same here. So lyrical is his language and oversized his characters, that some compare his setting to grand opera. With the broadest possible strokes, he outlines the fundamental moral drama of history, the conflict of good and evil. This is a biblical "Star Wars," a cosmic showdown. This is the high noon of the battle for human hearts.

The Woman and the Dragon (12:1-6)

A great sign appeared in the sky. We see a woman clothed with the sun, crowned with twelve stars, and the moon under her feet. She is pregnant and in labor to bring forth her son.

A second sign appeared. We see a flame red dragon, with seven crowned heads and ten horns. He stands in front of the woman to seize her baby and consume him.

Who is the woman? Answers vary. In her liturgy, the church uses this passage for the first reading for the feast of the glorious Assumption of Mary, identifying Mary with the woman. I believe this is the best interpretation of the identity of the woman. Mary was a real woman and a real mother. Her extraordinary surrender to God's will and her most intimate sharing in the mystery of salvation has attached to her a rich symbolism.

The details in this chapter bear that out. Mary is clothed with the symbols of creation — sun and stars. She stands on the moon, the sign of night. She is robed in light and controls the darkness under her feet. Like Eve who met the serpent, Mary encounters the dragon. Unlike Eve, who surrendered to the serpent's temptation, Mary surrendered to God and resisted all temptation. Like Eve, she is pregnant with new life. But Eve's children will be sinners.

Unlike Eve, Mary bears the sinless author of life. Her son will save all people from sin. Here, Mary, as the Woman, makes us think of the first creation, but also of the new creation in Jesus. In John's gospel, Jesus calls Mary "Woman" both at Cana and at the cross. Had he called her mother, he would be referring to her as his biological parent. By speaking to her as woman, he addresses her in her role as a unique participant in the process of salvation. Now the woman of John's gospel reappears as the woman in John's book of Revelation.

At the cross, Jesus made Mary the mother of the church when he said to John, "Behold, your mother" (Jn. 19:27). Mary, the woman in this vision, is both mother of the church and also a symbol of the church's own spiritual maternity that gives birth to all Christians in baptism. Mary personalizes what might otherwise be an abstract idea — the church both as institution and community. A person captivates the interest and imagination of the ordinary man and woman. An institution, even in its communal aspect, sounds too academic. Saints and heroines sum up cultures and nations in their lives. Mary does that for us when we want to appreciate the maternal call of the church.

The best way to understand the role and meaning of the woman in this vision is to see her as Mary. She wears the cosmic jewels and attire of the creation story. She replaces Eve, the physical mother of all sinners, by becoming the spiritual mother of the redeemed. She symbolizes the church's motherly role, helping us to experience the warmth of the church's truest vocation of begetting us as newborn Christians in Jesus Christ.

The Flame-Colored Dragon

Opposed to the woman is the dragon. This creature with seven crowned heads and ten horns stands before the woman and plans to devour her baby when he is born. Who is the dragon? John tells us that he is the devil, Satan, the leader of all the anti-God forces from Eden to the present day (cf. verse 9). Biblical thinkers associated Satan with the serpent that tempted Eve and the leviathan sea monster which inhabited the chaos out of which God made creation.

The Genesis creation story began with a scene of chaos, a vast void of nothingness and disorder. Biblical people (and other ancients as well) imagined that the leviathan was the lord of this frightening, watery darkness. The healing, creative word of God brought order and control out of this morass.

In the story of the temptation of Eve, the biblical writer characterized Satan as the serpent, an alter-ego of the leviathan, who lured Eve into the moral chaos and disorder of sin. The temptation event reversed the order of creation. God had moved chaos to cosmos (meaning physical and moral order). Now the serpent would move cosmos back to chaos/disorder. With the sin of Eve and Adam, the destructive possibilities of nature return. And for the first time the chaotic tragedy of human sinfulness arrives.

The dragon who appears before the woman is a combination of the leviathan and the serpent, the embodiment of physical and moral chaos. As the instigator of physical disorder, his tail sweeps away a third of the stars. As the incarnation of moral disorder, he plans to destroy the Savior who would be born of the woman. Behind this threatening image is a far more realistic and sinister reality, the devil.

The Devil

In our time we have relegated monsters to the stuff of nightmares. We soothe our fears away with horror stories in novels and films that make us laugh at our fears. We have learned how to banish the monster myths. We have gone further and done all we can to erase the belief in the existence of the devil as well. Having disposed of the monster image of the devil, we then proceeded to laugh away the reality of Satan pictured by the serpent and the dragon. Yes, monsters do not really exist. But, alas, the devil does. The apostle Peter writes that the devil, like a roaring lion, seeks to devour our spiritual integrity and rob us of the gift of salvation (I Pt. 5:8). We have no reason to believe any differently than Peter. Are we more enlightened than Peter? Today we have no reason to believe or behave any differently than he did. Satan succeeded with Adam and Eve. Why do we think this angel of death cannot succeed with us?

The biblical writers used the mythologies of their times to

describe the war between good and evil. The myths used monsters and gods to illustrate the conflict. Today there are new mythologies to dramatize the same story. This accounts for the popularity of the Star Trek and Star Wars films. The setting is cosmic. The monsters are the strange-looking creatures who use the awesome powers of modern technology to blast goodness away. When it is most honest about itself, human nature knows that the basic goal in life is the conquest of evil and self-destructive forces. Despite the denials of our culture, people know in their heart of hearts that evil is real and it should be fought against.

Biblical realism compels us to face non-physical realities. Indeed that is the key — "realities." Modern life would have us believe that the only things that are real are what can be tasted, seen, felt, touched, heard, smelled. This is called empiricism. Only what can be scientifically demonstrated is real. The Bible reminds us that heavenly beings are real. It also teaches that hellish beings are real too. Read with faith, Scripture is a mind-altering experience that calls us to expand our appreciation of what stands for the real. Our modern mentality would deny reality to anything that cannot be physically proven. But the modern mind is wrong on this issue.

We should never dismiss the Book of Revelation as a kind of scriptural science fiction. The dreamlike pictures stand for beings and truths that are very real indeed. The modern mind wants to reduce all reality to the physical and measurable. It is minimalist and restrictive. That is why it fills us with loss of self-worth and despair. Scripture expands consciousness to embrace the whole world of the spirit. It is maximalist and creative. That is why it fills us with self-confidence and hope. The culture imprisons us in the tiny cell of the self. Scripture liberates us to roam the universe of freedom. The culture makes us tongue-tied. Scripture opens our lips to sing with a roar of praise.

So now we see on the canvas of history the confrontation of the woman and the dragon. The woman bears a Son who will rule the nations with a rod of iron (cf. Ps. 2:9). This is clearly Jesus Christ, our savior and messiah. John writes that this Son goes immediately to the throne of God. This refers to the resurrection and ascension of Jesus. There is no reason here to speak of his earthly ministry or passion and death. That is assumed. What must be stressed is Christ's victory over sin and death as made visible in his glorious resurrection and ascension into heaven. In this brief line is explained the victory of the woman's Son over the dragon. More will be said about this in John's description of the fallen angels, but first he speaks to the condition of the church on earth.

He says the woman fled to the desert for 1,260 days (cf. Dn. 7:25). Here Mary symbolizes the church which is enduring a period of purification, first under the Romans and then under the various persecutors who will afflict her until the end of time. The 1,260 days, or three and a half years of persecution, is a symbolic way of talking about eras of purification in which the church lives out the mystery of the cross. Each period of persecution is an occasion of growth in the holiness of the church. The suffering washes away the greed and self-centeredness that is so self-destructive.

The Real Star Wars (12:7-12)

Remember that Revelation should be read as teaching us about three levels of history. First, about the condition of the infant church in John's time. That church needs encouragement in its battle against the "Dragon-Roman Empire," which for it is an incarnation of Satan's will to destroy Christ. Secondly, Revelation speaks to our own modern history both to well-known experiences of the persecution of our church as well as to our personal battles with physical and spiritual evil. We also need spiritual encouragement. Thirdly, Revelation moves us forward to the end of time when there will be one final confrontation between the Body of Christ and the forces of evil, led by Satan. Spiritual hope will be needed then as well.

With this in mind, we join John in looking at warfare between the good angels led by Michael and the bad angels led by Satan. Michael and the good angels won the battle. "The huge dragon, the ancient serpent, who is called the Devil and Satan, who deceived the whole world, was thrown down to earth, and its angels were thrown down with it" (verse 9). The prophet Isaiah alluded to such a conflict. "How you have fallen from the heavens, O morning star!"

(Is. 14:12). Another name for the "morning star" is Lucifer, the light carrier. Jesus echoed this, "I have observed Satan fall like lightning from the sky" (Lk. 10:18).

What was the sin of the evil angels? Having no bodies or physical passions, they could not sin by means of physical violence or lust. The only way they could rebel against God was through the spiritual sins of pride and envy. They could become so enchanted with their own marvelous gifts that they could be persuaded they are the source of their own goodness. They could be led to envy God and deny that the Lord was the giver of their wondrous qualities.

John describes their temptation to pride in terms of battle imagery. Because they were angels, they would not have frequent temptations, just one profound seduction, one chance to choose God. They faced that one moment of trial. One group chose God and went on to enjoy forever the heavenly goal to which they were called. The other group rebelled against God and fell from grace. Pride hurled them down from heaven past all the ranks of the good angels, even past all of earth's humans from the saints to the sinners.

God has permitted them — now called devils — to tempt us to the same spiritual pride and all its related sins. We are free to resist them. We have the power of the Holy Spirit to defend us against them. God has also permitted them to work through evil people on earth to destroy the church, but God has also sent the Holy Spirit to stand with the church against all the "gates of hell."

The warfare in heaven that John would have us inspect is now going on here on earth, both between the church and its enemies and between ourselves and the hostile forces of evil. Each one of us personally is engaged in a spiritual combat. If we have lost the sense of this, that is because the culture and our own weakness has dulled our perceptions. The New Testament and all of church history has huge amounts of testimony about spiritual warfare and how to deal with it. The absence of a consciousness of this in our own day is not because the battle does not exist. It is evidence that we are letting the forces of evil make us believe there is no war to be fought.

When even Jesus himself was tempted and wrestled with the devil for forty days in the desert, do we think we are absolved from such a moral struggle? What goes on globally also goes on in each human soul. John holds up for us the example of the martyrs who won the fight with evil and conquered it by the power of the Lamb. We hear their song of triumph even as they lose their lives for Christ. "Love for life did not deter them from death (that is, dying for their faith)" (verse 11).

The Dragon Pursues the Church (12:13-18)

At the same time John alerts the people of God that the "Devil has come down to you in great fury" (verse 12). Why? To make us be as miserable as he is, to make us refuse salvation. God gives the woman — that is, the church — the eagle wings of grace during her days in the desert of persecution and temptation. She has the power to fly from temptation and the grace to endure the onslaught for 1,260 days, meaning the period between the Ascension and Christ's Second Coming.

The dragon/serpent/Satan "spewed a torrent of water out of his mouth after the woman to sweep her away with the current" (verse 15). This is an attempt to move all creation back to the chaos and the formless void described in the first verses of the Bible. The torrent of water is an image of the dark ocean out of which God is pictured as beginning creation. The dragon wants a counter-creation, a reversal of the divine plan of love.

"Then the dragon became angry with the woman and went off to wage war against the rest of her offspring, those who keep God's commandments and bear witness to Jesus" (verse 17). What the dragon wants to do to the church in general, it also wants to accomplish with her individual, faithful members. In other words, to each of us. If we remain in vigorous and faithful communion with the church, we will share in her resistance to evil. If we stay close to the woman, Mary the God-bearer, we will have the energy and dynamism to stand against the power of evil.

Our intimacy with the church and Mary will guarantee an intimacy with Jesus and the power of the Holy Spirit. This is a warfare that requires spiritual weapons. The "eagle wings" of grace are as available to us as to the church, for we are the members of the Body of Christ.

As we conclude our meditation on this first part of the spiritual warfare depicted by John, we must draw up an action plan for our own lives. I suggest the following strategy.

Become Conscious of the Aggressiveness of Evil. The tendency today is to reduce the causes of evil to psychological and social reasons. While there is a lot of truth to this analysis, it is not deep enough. Moreover, it sometimes moves us to excuse ourselves from responsibility for our unhappiness. Emotional or psychological pain is a cause of evil. Economic misery and political oppression are sociological causes of evil. But to blame parents for our troubles is not a good solution to our feelings of sorrow. Or to claim that seeking sexual freedom from all restraints is the solution to personal emotional grief is a false message. Moreover, to blame the system for our economic ills is an insufficient response to our lamentable condition. Therapy for our emotional ills and revolt for our social sorrows are inadequate responses.

What we need is a biblical anthropology, a deeper view of who we are and the real reason why evil happens to us. God created us in his own image. He gave us a mind, a will, emotions, and a body. He also stamped within us an orderly plan for our happiness. The body should be ordered upward to the rule of the soul. The emotions ought to be under the control of the will. And the will should be obedient to the mind. The mind ought to be obedient to God. When we live by this orderly plan for us, we will move toward peace and happiness. When we refuse to do so, we have troubles.

Because of original sin, the mind is darkened, the will is weak, and the passions are like wild adolescents. Because of the aggressiveness of evil, in the person of Satan, we are also at risk spiritually. Seen from this point of view, we appear to be so vulnerable; we could wonder if we would have any chance against our own disorder, let alone against the brilliance of a fallen angel.

If it were not for Jesus Christ, we would have cause to despair. But his saving work in Galilee and on Calvary, and in his glorification, his sending of the Spirit, and the foundation of the church and the sacraments assure us that we have both a positive direction and the spiritual means to live by it.

I have said that psychological and sociological reasons do not sufficiently account for our human condition. Behind them lie the forces of original and actual sin and the powers of diabolical evil.

But we have no reason to be afraid. We can overcome. The only thing we should fear today is the illusion that there is no spiritual warfare going on against us. The greatest triumph of evil is to make us think there is no evil. One of the supreme benefits of studying Revelation is the awareness it raises of the true state of things in the world and in our souls.

The cure for our spiritual disease is the obedience of faith. We tend to think of faith only as an intellectual assent to divine revelation. But faith is also a matter of the action of our wills. Living our faith means being obedient to Christ and his plan for our happiness. Spiritual pride is the worst sin because it makes us disobey God's plan for our happiness. Spiritual humility is the greatest virtue because it makes us obey God's plan for our happiness.

So the warfare that once went on in heaven between Michael and the good angels and Lucifer and the bad ones now goes on within our own personal lives. Each of us is the setting where that primordial battle is fought. At the base of the psychological torment we face is the choice between order and disorder in our souls. At the root of the sociological misery we encounter are the sinful economic and political decisions to enforce chaos on us in the public square.

Until we realize the spiritual and moral roots of all that happens to us personally and socially, we will miss the truth of what is going on in our lives and the world. Evil is not shy about hitting us aggressively. We should not be bashful about striking back with all the force of the cross, the strength of Jesus, and the power of the Spirit.

Reflection

1. How does my devotion to Mary help me to be devoted to the church?
2. Why is it possible to say that the sufferings of the church, like that of a woman in labor, are the birth pangs of the church?
3. What has been the development of my thinking about the devil

and his evil influence on my life?

4. Why are psychology and sociology, important as they are, inadequate explanations of and solutions to the evil I experience?

5. What is the biblical explanation of who I am and why I tend toward evil? What should I do about it?

6. Why does the world make me think there is no evil tendency within my heart and no force of evil outside me intent on corrupting me?

7. What is the impact on me of the images in this twelfth chapter — images of the woman, the dragon, the warfare in heaven, the violent attack on the woman and her child?

8. What are the leading indicators of hope in this chapter?

9. What connection could I make between the woman and the dragon and Our Lady of Fatima and Communism?

10. Why is Mary's intercession so powerful for the church?

Prayer

Jesus, messiah and savior, you have won the victory over Satan and evil. Yet each of us in our own history must experience that victory of yours by undergoing the specific trials and temptations that come to us. We cannot do it without your graces and your Spirit. We prayerfully trust in your Mother's intercession, the woman who bore you, the woman who symbolizes the church. Awaken us to our moral and spiritual calling. Alert us to our inner evil tendencies and the outer temptations of Satan. Save us, Jesus. Now.

13 Who Is the Beast? The Antichrist

When the world is in trouble it looks for a savior. Years ago, the historian Arnold Toynbee wrote, "The nations are now ready to give the kingdoms of the world to any one man who will offer a solution to the world's problems."

Paul-Henri Charles Spaak, one of the early planners of the European Common Market, said, "We do not want another committee, we have too many already. What we want is a man of sufficient stature to hold the allegiance of all the people and to lift us up out of the economic morass into which we are sinking. Send us such a man, and be he God or be he the Devil, we will receive him."

This is a dangerous desire as the evidence of the twentieth century has proven. Nazi Germany answered this need with Hitler. Communist Russia responded to this hunger with Lenin and Stalin. People looked for a god and settled for a devil. These men easily fulfilled the description of the beast found in this chapter.

Catastrophic times cause people to search for a savior. The mistake they usually make is to quest for such a person among human candidates. Instead of turning to the God-man, Jesus, who calls each person to moral and spiritual conversion as the condition for salvation, millions of people surrender their freedom and responsibility to a tyrant. The result in our times was the worst hot war in history (World War II) and forty years of cold war after that with the Soviet Union.

For nearly a half century, money, energy, and human resources were devoted to war in one form or another instead of peace. Such is the price of putting our faith in a purely human solution to our problems. The "beasts" of Nazi Germany and Communist Russia were anti-God leaders. They were case studies in what Scripture calls the Antichrist. They murdered millions of believers, suppressed religion, and subordinated faith in God to belief in the state. Small wonder the psalmist says, "Put not your trust in princes" (Ps. 146:3).

That tragic era is behind us. But a so-called "new world order" has begun. In fact it is not order but instability. As we move toward the year 2000, the celebration of the third millennium of the advent of Jesus Christ, our real Savior, this instability will cause new appeals for a strong human leader to save us from true and imagined woes.

People will again thirst for a charismatic super-leader. What they are likely to get is another version of Satan's Superman, the beast of the Apocalypse, another Antichrist. But unless there is prayer, penance and personal religious conversion, we are destined to make the same mistakes as those who went before us.

The Leviathan — The Beast From the Sea (13:1-10)

Chapter 13 of Revelation gives us a powerful description of the Antichrist under the image of the beast. In the first ten verses we see the beast as a monster from the sea. In the last eight verses we see another picture of the beast as a monster from the land. It is the same person in both cases, Satan in disguise. In reality, for John, this devil-incarnate is Nero, the Roman beast-emperor. But the image also applies to all the cruel tyrants of history who have brutalized human beings and sought to destroy the love, mercy, and justice of God on earth. Lastly, such a beast will appear at the end of time just before the last judgment.

Millenarians, people always on the outlook for the end of the world, frequently believe they have spotted the ultimate beast. That will surely occur in our own day as the nervous fervor accompanying the arrival of the year 2000 comes upon us. They are perfect examples of what Jesus predicted about how humans will act at the end of time. "If anyone says to you then, 'Look, here is the Messiah!' or 'There he is!,' do not believe it. False messiahs and false prophets will arise, and will perform signs and wonders so great as to deceive, if that were possible, even the elect" (Mt. 24:23-24).

Christ's prediction is difficult to apply to any one period of history because what he foresaw has occurred in many ages of world crisis. What he said will indeed apply to the actual end of the world. It also happens to be true of any time of extreme turmoil and confusion. We can now see in retrospect that his prediction fits not just the final end of the world, but also any eras of immense stress for the world and the church.

But fundamentalist millenarians prefer to control his words and seek literal fulfillment in their own times. They forget the other cautionary words of Jesus about not knowing the precise time of the end. "But of that day or hour no one knows, neither the angels of heaven, nor the Son, but the Father alone" (Mt. 24:36). Jesus was basically saying that it was not important to know the exact date of the end of the world, but rather to be prepared at any time in our personal lives for the coming of the Lord, whether that be our sudden or lingering death (the end of our own personal world) or the historical end of time. "You also must be prepared, for at an hour you do not expect, the Son of Man will come" (Mt. 24:44).

Despite Christ's warnings, fundamentalist millenarians will scan today's political developments to convince us that the end is now surely near. They will cite the restoration of Israel as a sign. They will note the possibility of rebuilding the Third Temple in Jerusalem as a sign. Even the rise of Iraq will be evidence. They will adduce all kinds of biblical prophecies from Ezekiel, Daniel, and the Book of Revelation to support their argument. But if Jesus tells us we will never know the day or the hour, that is what should be our position.

In the face of global insecurity and instability, the important spiritual application is the quality of our spiritual and moral lives. That is what should concern us no matter how unsettling the state of the world. In fact, because of that confusion, we should be motivated strongly to put our lives in order. Secondly, we should renew our faith in the victory of the Lamb over the beast.

Instead of shuddering fearfully about the sad state of world affairs, we ought to renew our confidence in the power of the cross and the resurrection of Jesus Christ. With the confidence that comes from this faith and spiritual revitalization, we then can undertake efforts — empowered with God's grace — to put our souls and our world in order. We have already seen this message in John's letters to the seven churches in chapters 2-3 of Revelation.

Who then is this beast from the sea in the first ten verses of this chapter? It is simply another version of the dragon who is an image of Satan and the Devil (Rev. 12:9). I have already explained the use of this imagery in the meditation on chapter 12. The sea is the chaos, the formless void or nothingness described in the first verses of Genesis. Biblical imagination pictured it as ruled by a sea monster, the leviathan. In religious terms this means that Satan is the lord of chaos fighting against the created order/cosmos of God. It is God's will that nature should be orderly and that human nature should be just as ordered in the moral and spiritual sense. The beast from the sea wants to reduce the world to confusion and disorder — and to erode the human soul into moral chaos.

What then is new in this chapter? Why does John linger on the mission of the beast? Because in chapter 12 the attention is mainly on the cosmic battle between good and evil, between the Woman and the Dragon, between the Body of Christ and Satan, while here the focus is on the incarnation of the beast in a human Antichrist. He is saying that the beast will become a divinized tyrant with awesome powers and its own earthly throne.

This beast will have adoring followers. "Fascinated, the whole world followed after the beast. . . . They also worshiped the beast and said, 'Who can compare with the beast or who can fight against it' " (verses 3-4). We have already seen this in contemporary history with the personality cults of Hitler, Mao, Stalin, and more recently, with Saddam Hussein. Their giant pictures and statues were everywhere in their countries. The outstretched right arms of millions accompanied roars of adulation. At one point over half the human race was in bondage to this new form of idolatry. Over a billion people still are as of this writing. John names this for what it really is — blasphemy. Adoring a human being as a god. Through the lips of billions the beast "opened its mouth to utter blasphemies against God" (verse 6). John was talking about Nero, but he was also prophetically accusing all the other Antichrists that have arisen since his time.

These Antichrists will be allowed to "wage war against the holy ones and conquer them" (verse 7). Roman emperors did this in the first century and dictators have done the same in our own day. But we have lived long enough to know their victory is temporary and illusory. The "holy ones" they persecuted kept the faith and many of them have survived to see the vindication of Christ. The brave Christians of Central and Eastern Europe, who endured and survived Communist oppression, are an example of the grace-filled tenacity of the "holy ones." "Such is the faithful endurance of the holy ones" (verse 10).

The Behemoth — The Beast From the Land (13:11-18)

In chapter 12 I showed how biblical writers adapted the mythologies of their times to illustrate the work of Satan. They used dragons, serpents, and leviathans to put across this point, just as we use science fiction myths today to dramatize the enduring conflict between good and evil. Here John is using yet another image familiar to his readers. The behemoth — an imaginary land monster — is another picture of Satan.

This time Satan appears, not as a political tyrant, but as a seductive false prophet. The leviathan was an external threat to the church. The behemoth is an internal one. It is easy to identify an enemy that sits on a throne and threatens torture and death to get compliance. It is confusing and difficult to name an enemy who seems to be our friend.

Jesus used a "down-home" image to alert us to this problem. "Beware of false prophets, who come to you in sheep's clothing, but underneath are ravenous wolves" (Mt. 7:15). Saint Paul echoed this teaching. "I know that after my departure savage wolves will come among you, and they will not spare the flock" (Acts 20:29). False prophets subvert the church from within.

In John's time the false prophets were of two kinds. We saw in his letters to the seven churches, he warned against listening to those members of the community who advocated sexual promiscuity in the name of Gospel freedom. Here he is making his people aware of the deceit of the priest representatives of the empire who used magic and other tricks as though they performed miracles with divine power. The beast "deceived the inhabitants of the earth with the signs it was allowed to perform" (verse 14).

Moreover, these pagan priests used sweet reason to convince

Christians it was just a small matter to burn a little incense before one of the numerous statues of the emperor that were to be found everywhere. After all, Rome had been good to them, protected them from fierce enemies, kept the peace and brought prosperity. What's a little incense? Of course, behind the carrot was the stick of death or economic punishment. Faithful Christians were not always martyred but neither were they stamped with the beast's "image on their right hands or their foreheads" (verse 16). This was probably a tatoo. The result was that unstamped Christians could not "buy or sell" (verse 17) meaning they could not run a business. Hence they were reduced to menial or slave status with the lowest possible income.

What is 666?

As a sign of love and fidelity the Lamb marked his followers on the forehead with the seal of the living God. "Do not damage the land or the seas or the trees until we put the seal on the foreheads of the servants of our God" (7:3).

Now the beast imitates the Lamb, marking his followers on the forehead or on the right hand. For John, there are only these two groups, these two choices. Everyone bears one mark or the other. There are to be no anonymous Christians, no middle of the road, no non-aligned.

John tells us that the mark of the beast is the number 666. For centuries this has been like a religious crossword puzzle, many scholars and religious hobbyists arguing over its decoding. The text says that the number stands for a person (verse 18). In John's time, the individual letters in Greek, Hebrew, and Latin also stood for a number. This means that every word could also be a numerical sum of its letters. Given this fact, the most widely accepted theory is that 666 stands for Neron Caesar which is *nrwn-qsr* in Hebrew (50 + 200 + 6 + 50 + 100 + 60 + 200). This only works if you put an "n" at the end of Nero's name (hence, Neron), which spelling conveniently was found in a Dead Sea scroll. If this be true then John is teaching that 666 is Nero and other harsh emperors like him.

Application

I have already drawn several lessons from this chapter. (1) We should avoid the tendency of the fundamentalist millenarians who try to name specific dates for the end of the world. This will become increasingly popular as the year 2000 approaches. (2) The church can expect periodic persecutions from authoritarian leaders, as is still the truth in China and Vietnam and, increasingly, in some Islamic fundamentalist countries. For example, Christianity is forbidden in Saudi Arabia. Legal punishments for Christian practice are in effect. (3) The church will also be threatened by false prophets from within. This last point deserves some more reflection here.

This is the "sheep in wolves' clothing" approach. It is no secret that there are people "in good standing" who use their office and professional degrees to justify teachings that are opposed to the Magisterium. Some of them openly encourage hostile attitudes and practices toward the pope. In speaking of similar problems in his day (late sixteenth to early seventeenth century), St. Robert Bellarmine said that, while he often agreed with some of the genuine insights of such people, he would not approve their sermons, lectures, or writings because they were instigating opposition to the chief shepherd of the church.

It must be clearly understood that the people in question constitute a relatively small, but influential minority. Most of our members are faith-filled people, intent on doing God's will and positive about the church.

Today we have some who say that "experience" is the most important thing. If church teaching says something different, then the teaching must be changed. They want to accommodate the culture, not challenge it with Christ's teachings. A professor of Christology makes the claim that Christians do not need to have a personal relationship with Christ and that suffering has no value. Such a position substitutes personal judgment for that of Christ, the church fathers, all of authentic Christian tradition, and the present Magisterium.

People such as these preach from some of our pulpits and teach in some of our classrooms. They are false prophets, using their approved church positions to publicly undermine the church. In the name of openness, they would close the Catholic mind to the real truth of Jesus. Under the guise of professional competence they would lure us from what we thought to be true and persuade us to accept a lie.

We are tempted to speak sedately and politely about these aberrations in our church. Civil discourse forbids us from using colorful language to criticize them. John is not cautious about the false prophets of his day. He calls them the beast, the land monster who would use a soft sell to seduce people from their faith. I agree with John. I think we should not sit back and let false prophets delude the faithful members of the church. We should be alert and critical when we hear such people.

We should call their bluff and expose their strategy. We should do this with the simplicity of the dove and the cunning of the serpent. Our motive must be the love of Christ and the church. Our church and our faith is too precious to be left to the careless enmity of false prophets. Let us trust in the true prophet — the pope and the Magisterium to guide us.

At the same time, in the spirit of Christ's forgiveness, we should pray for the conversion of heart of those who would divide the church. All during his ministry Jesus reached out to those who were alienated from him or turned against him. At the Last Supper Jesus prayed for the unity of the church. St. Francis asks us to pray, "Let me be a channel of your peace." Our prayer that false shepherds be reconciled with the church is especially needed in our day.

Reflection

1. How would I deal with people who try to convince me that they know the exact date of the end of the world?
2. In times of crisis some may say, "Send us a savior. Be he a god or a devil we would receive him." What would I say?
3. If I were explaining Revelation to others, how would I teach them about the dragon, the serpent, the leviathan, and the behemoth?
4. What "mythical stories" could I use today to explain the conflict between good and evil?

5. How could I apply the image of the beast from the sea to historical events of this century?
6. Who does the term "Antichrist" make me think of?
7. How should I respond to the preaching, teaching, and writing of "false shepherds" today?
8. Why is it important that in times of crisis in the church I try to be a channel of Christ's peace and reconciliation?
9. Why should I expect to hear a lot about the end of the world as the year 2000 approaches?
10. The beast marked his own with a sign. How does Jesus mark us as his own?

Prayer

Dear Jesus, when confusion mounts and crisis comes, help me to keep my wits about me. Make me a center of peace in the midst of conflict. Heal my heart of bitterness when I feel much to be angry about. Fill my mind with truth when I encounter deception. Reinforce my heart with love when I confront hatred. May I bring joy to those who are sad, hope to the despairing, and light to those in darkness. Give me your Holy Spirit to make this possible.

14 The Mystery Reveals and Conceals

Marked With Jesus (14:1-5)

The image of the beast dominated the last two chapters. The dragon threatened the woman. The leviathan from the sea — as Antichrist — besieged the worried Christian community. The behemoth from the land — as the false prophet — tried to subvert the church from within. We have seen how this applied to John's time as well as our own.

Now the image of the Lamb returns. The Lamb stands on Mount Zion surrounded by 144,000 Christians who have been marked with the Father's name written on their foreheads. The number is symbolic, representing both a large number of people as well as a reference to their outstanding fidelity.

The 144,000 is one of Scripture's "perfect" numbers, others being three, seven, and twelve, with their multiples. This does not refer here to absolute perfection which is only found in God. It speaks rather of the relative goodness, holiness, and wholeness of those marked with God's name, that is, with gifts of grace according to their openness to God's Spirit.

In Scripture, a physical sign or mark on one's body signified personal commitment or ownership. Soldiers wore tatoos to illustrate their loyalty to the emperor. Masters branded their slaves just as farmers would brand cattle. After Cain killed Abel he received some kind of a mark on his forehead to identify him as a murderer.

Throughout history Jews were sometimes forced to wear a mark to identify them. The Nazis were not the first ones to make them wear a Star of David on an arm band. In the concentration camps, all people were forced to accept a tattooed number on their wrists.

In our own society "marks" can be found everywhere. Today we call them "logos." NBC has the peacock. Automobile companies have their distinctive trademarks. The armed forces have uniforms to distinguish one from another.

For Christians the greatest mark of all is the cross. St. Paul said, "I bear the marks of Jesus on my body" (Gal. 6:17). Possibly he bore the stigmata, the wounds of Jesus on his wrists, feet, and side, such as happened to St. Francis of Assisi and other saints. Millions of Christians wear the cross on a chain around their necks. In other words the repeated use of the image of a mark in Revelation is not all that unusual, even today. People like to wear external symbols to indicate their beliefs, attitudes, and commitments.

What does God's Voice Sound Like?

Because none of us has ever been in heaven, we will never know exactly what is going on there. We can only use human comparisons. Jesus loved to use joyful wedding dinners to describe life in heaven. However, a comparison is not the same as the reality. That is why our words fumble and tumble when we want to share with another a memorable experience we have had. We finally settle for, "Well, you just should have been there."

St. Paul was given a glimpse of heaven. Listen to what he has to say about it. "I . . . was caught up into Paradise and heard ineffable things, which no one may utter" (II Cor. 12:3). So magnificent was this experience, so beyond human comprehension that Paul advises, "No eye has seen, nor ear heard, nor the heart of man conceived what God has prepared for those who love him" (I Cor. 2:9 RSV). In other words the mystery we proclaim remains essentially a mystery of faith.

Paul follows his own counsel. He would seem to say, "Whereof man cannot speak, thereof let him be silent." John, however, is aware there is a hunger for some notion of what the heavenly kingdom is like. We have an excellent idea of what God is like because Jesus came and showed us personally. For heaven we rely on comparisons.

In Revelation John employs a vast array of images to help us grasp the reality of heaven. So long as we realize that the image is not quite the same as the reality, we have a lovely series of pictures that give us a hint of the glory to come. Paul's caution reminds us of the hiddenness of the mystery. John's ebullience assures us we can sense something of what awaits us. The mystery reveals something. It also conceals a lot.

So, when I raise the question, "What does God's voice sound like?" I ask it in the context of a mystery that both reveals and conceals. John says God's voice is like the roar of a waterfall, or a clap of thunder, or the honey-soaked sound of harps (verse 2). His voice is at once awesome and yet enormously appealing. He has a sound that is alternately a bit scary like the crash of thunder and as sweetly intimate as a love song. God is not easily categorized or put in a box for our satisfaction. God is far more than anything we can say about him.

The greatest impression given here is that of music — a heavenly choir accompanied by harps. This is the reason why so much classical art and popular greeting cards show heaven with choirs and angels and harpists. These are little more than clues to the wonder of heaven itself. The pictures are meant to communicate the reality of heaven, its beauty and love. In fact heaven will even be far better than the most breathtaking beauty we have ever experienced.

Who Are the Virgins?

Verse 4 says that a host of "virgins" echoed the music of the angels. Who are the virgins? These are the people who did not adore the beast. They did not succumb to the temptation of idolatry. They did not kneel before the statue of the emperor or kiss its toe or burn incense before it. The verse does not refer to virgins in the strict sense of the word, that is, to women who have never married or had sex.

Scripture uses the image of a virgin to describe fidelity to God. Idolatry is associated with prostitution. The Hebrew word for adultery can also mean idolatry. The Book of Revelation says Babylon is a whore. "Babylon the great, the mother of harlots" (Rev. 17:4). But the church is the faithful (virginal) spouse of the Lamb. "For the wedding day of the Lamb has come, his bride (the virginal/faithful church) has made herself ready" (Rev. 19:7).

At the same time actual celibacy and virginity as a spiritual calling already existed in New Testament times. Jesus and Paul extolled the value of marriage and its spiritual meaning. Yet both men were celibates. Tradition also says that the apostle John was celibate. Our Blessed Mother, though married, always remained a virgin. God calls most people to marriage and some people to celibacy and virginity. That was true in the beginning and remains true today. Virginity still remains a symbol of faithfulness to Christ, and it was that symbolic meaning John used in this verse 4 of Revelation.

Three Angelic Messages (14:6-13)

Next John tells us of three angels and their messages. The first one proclaims Good News or Gospel to the whole world. This angel urges us to fear God, give him glory, and worship him. There is good fear and bad fear. Good fear is a gift of the Holy Spirit. This is the fear of one who loves God and is afraid of losing this relationship. The more I love God the more I fear losing my contact with him. This fear begets wisdom in me because I realize how precious is my friendship with God and I will do all I can to maintain it.

Bad fear is my reluctance to enter into a relationship with God or anyone else. Bad fear makes me dislike the responsibility that is necessary for love. Bad fear restricts my outlook and makes me timid about relating to others. I am afraid of the risk of love and I dread being let down or betrayed.

This is why Scripture tells so many stories of letting go of fear whenever heaven contacts earth. The angel told Mary not to be afraid at the Annunciation. Jesus commands the apostles not to be scared in the upper room on Easter night. The Gospel is Good News taking away bad fear. It never eliminates good fear which motivates us to avoid any sin that would separate us from loving and being loved by Christ.

The second angel announces that Babylon will fall and disappear. This Babylon is a whore that made the world drink "the wine of her licentious passions" (verse 8). John contrasts Babylon (code word for imperial Rome here) with the virginal fidelity of the church. The angel is a sign of hope for the suffering church. Despite all appearances this evil empire will crumble. It happened in ancient times. It has happened in our own.

The third angel tells the world that all those who worship evil will go to hell. Unrepentant sinners will "drink the wine of God's fury. . . . The smoke of the fire that torments them will rise forever and ever" (verses 10-11). Biblical realism does not avoid the reality of eternal punishment for unrepentant sinners. God's love can conquer sin and death.

But God will not force any sinner to change. Sinners have freedom. If they choose evil they will come to an evil end and an evil destiny. Scripture's words are not tame. Sinners will be "tormented in burning sulphur" (verse 10). While these physical images should not be taken literally, their spiritual meaning should not be denied. A hell of everlasting pain exists. We may not know the exact nature of that suffering. We do know that unrepentant sinners will suffer it forever.

Contrast this with the angel's words of assurance for the just who stayed close to God. "Blessed are the dead who die in the Lord. . . . Let them find rest from their labors" (verse 13).

The Wheat of Salvation — The Grapes of Wrath (14:14-20)

These final verses are typical biblical pictures of the Last Judgment. The harvest of wheat is the gathering of the saved. The harvest of grapes is the assembling of the damned. They will be thrown into God's winepress, trodden down outside the city until their blood flows "to the height of a horse's bridle for two hundred miles" (verse 20).

The judge comes on a white cloud and is similar to one who looked like a son of man — or simply a man. This image of judgment can be found in Daniel 7:13-14 and again in Matthew 24:30. Daniel predicted that the messiah would come to judge the world. Matthew tells us that Jesus is the one who will do this. Here John simply repeats what would be well known to his listeners.

It is not clear why Scripture here uses wheat to symbolize the saved and grapes to stand for the damned. Jesus had done very much the same. He saw a wheat field and envisioned it as the site for harvesting souls for salvation. When he talked about evil people he sometimes use parables about vineyards and winepresses. It may have something to do with the innocence of bread and the potential excesses of wine. The wine cult of Dionysius — with its orgies and drunken abandon — may have something to do with this usage.

Yet Jesus also used both bread and wine (fruit of the grain and the grape) as the materials for the Eucharist. Symbolic use of wheat and grapes therefore can have divergent meanings depending on the situation.

This chapter closes on a note of judgment. The focus is on the divine judge. At the same time it should be said that we are responsible for our destinies. If we choose love and God we will gain eternal life. If we choose evil and the "beast" we will experience eternal death. As we live so shall we die. Christ the judge confirms what we have already done to ourselves.

What Does This Mean for Us?

Chapters 12-14 are the heart of the book of Revelation. They summarize all that went before. They foresee all that will be said hereafter. By the standards of our sanitized, approved language today, the verses seem wild and perhaps even out of control. Do we like to hear of two hundred miles of blood as high as a horse's bridle? Do we rush over descriptions of the punishments of the damned, drowned in sulphur, choking on smoke, and burning in fire?

Yet in our own times the violence of life is showing up in our language. Popular novels are filled with blasphemies and four-letter words. Numerous films both in theaters and on TV ring with blue talk and unrestrained angry outbursts. We seem no longer surprised that even our little children can "curse a blue streak." We have become increasingly tolerant of the violent language of sinners — all in the name of freedom of speech.

Yet we would not dream of using the kind of biblical language found in Revelation to speak of unrepentant sinners. Preachers who would dare to use "fire and brimstone" talk would be laughed out of the pulpit. Strange is it not? We protect the freedom of those who pollute our ears and eyes with the conversation of sin. We deny the use of Scripture's colorful language of judgment for unrepentant sinners.

Now it is true that this biblical approach is still alive and well on the lips of some fundamentalist radio, TV, and street preachers. They, too, are ridiculed and put down for their ignorance and ranting. I have to say that I agree with the resistance to them. Their perspective is too narrow. There is not nearly enough of the love of God and the joyful message of the Good News of Jesus.

What we need is a balance. Jesus, Paul, and the apostles spent most of their time explaining the offer of forgiveness and the joys of love and virtue and the power of grace to their listeners. Proportionately, they spent little of their time and energy using condemnatory talk. But they were not above it. Christ's Last Judgment sermons appear in the gospels. The epistles are firm about the judgment that will come to unrepentant sinners. There is room for this amid all the feel-good talk we hear in the church today. A dose of biblical realism will not hurt any of us.

No writer of the New Testament did a better job of talking about love than John. Yet he is the same one who gives us the judgment talk of Revelation. He reminds us we should listen to the whole story of Scripture, not just the parts we like. Good news only makes sense to those caught by bad news. A balanced approach is better than any extreme.

Reflection

1. A detective story is called a mystery story. Why?
2. How would the comparison of a mystery story apply to our understanding of heaven?
3. If I were to hear God's voice what would I imagine it sounded like?
4. The term "mark" appears frequently in Revelation. What are examples of marks or logos today?
5. Older catechisms spoke of the baptismal character as a mark on our soul. What would Revelation teach us about this?

6. What is my reaction to the violent language about the punishment of the damned in this chapter?
7. Our meditation on this chapter speaks about good and bad fear. What is the role of fear in my faith life?
8. What do I think about the Last Judgment?
9. How would I react to a "fire and brimstone" homily at my parish church?
10. How do I react to the violent language on TV, films, and in popular writing today?

Prayer

Lord Jesus, you loved us so deeply that you took some of the mystery out of our understanding of God. You revealed so much truth and light that I will need a lifetime to absorb it and practice it. At the same time, there is so much more to your mystery. I will only know that when, by your grace, I am with you in heaven. Keep me firm in faith and loyalty to you so I may be part of the "wheat harvest" at the judgment.

15 A Sea of Glass Touched With Fire

The Song of the Redeemed (15:1-8)

Everyone is familiar with the ten plagues of Egypt which were followed by the crossing of the Red Sea. Here John reworks that ancient event and reverses the order. The victorious Christians cross the sea of glass to freedom. Then come the plagues upon the enemies of God's people. John may have borrowed his image of the sea of glass from his vantage point on the island of Patmos. From time to time when the sea was calm it looked like crystal. Clearly he adapted the Exodus story of the plagues to apply to the divine punishment that would come upon the Roman persecutors of the Christian church.

The sea of glass was mingled with fire. The image may be derived from the still surface of the water reflecting the fire of the sun. The army of the redeemed stands on the sea of glass. Accompanied by harps they sang the song of Moses and of the Lamb. The martyrs have come safely through the sea of persecution and have arrived at the shore of heaven.

One of the fascinating features of Revelation is the recurrence of exultant hymns of praise. Despite their suffering, the Christian community persists in breaking out in songs of adoration and thanksgiving. There is a liturgical quality to the whole book. The Christian heirs of Israel's psalmody and canticles carry forward the magnificent musical tradition noted in the Song of Moses, the psalms of David, and the canticles of various praise singers.

The hymns which John places in Revelation were most likely the ones used in the seven churches to whom he wrote in the early chapters of this book. Their words and melodies would arise from the Christian Eucharists. The texts both announce the "death of the

Lord" as well as his resurrected presence among them.

These "hymns of hope" sustained their hearts throughout the lengthy persecution described in this book. Great composers have mined them for inspiring new compositions throughout the centuries. The greatest among these was George Frideric Handel whose "Hallelujah Chorus," "Amen Chorus," and "Worthy is the Lamb" anthem are the most memorable and recognizable adaptations of hymnody in Revelation.

The Temple of Glory

Next John has a vision of the Jerusalem temple, transposed to heaven itself. He saw seven angels come from the "tent of testimony." When the Old Testament Hebrews were a nomadic people, they had a special shrine tent in which they set up the Ark of the Covenant. This chest, made of precious wood, contained the stone tablets of the ten commandments and some remains of the manna.

A gold lid covered the box. The people called it the "kipporeth," that is, the mercy seat, or throne of the compassionate God. Golden angels in the posture of adoration were placed on top of the ark. Their wings came up over their heads and nearly touched over the center of the ark. The empty space between the tips of the wings symbolized the presence of the invisible God. Sometimes the people beheld a shining cloud resting on the kipporeth-mercy seat. This was an apparition of God. That is why the people called the ark the throne of God.

In their post-nomadic history, the people built a temple in Jerusalem and installed the ark in the Holy of Holies, the name for the most sacred room inside the temple building. So the "tent of testimony" became the Holy of Holies. The use of the expression "testimony" referred to God's witnessing his visible presence to his people.

John beheld angels coming out of the tent of testimony (the Holy of Holies). They were dressed in clean white linen with a golden sash around their chests. In scriptural history these were the garments of both priests and kings. In the early days of the monarchy, kings often functioned as priests. Israel was a theocratic society in which the king was both a political and religious leader. In this scene the angels are clothed in priestly and royal garments.

One of the four living creatures gave each of the seven angels a bowl filled with the wrath of God. The temple filled with incense smoke — the cloud of God's glory. Here again is a typical symbol of God's presence popular in Old Testament days. God — as a pillar of fire by night and a pillar of cloud by day — had led Israel through the desert. Often God, appearing as a shining cloud, rested on the ark. Israel called this shining cloud, the "glory." The Hebrew word for glory is Shekinah. Hence, the use of the term glory in Scripture means the religious experience of God's presence.

Glory makes us think of God in terms of his beauty. But in this passage the splendor of God is matched with his wrath, his awesome power. God is infinite energy as well as limitless magnificence. The power of God can be used positively on behalf of liberating the Christian people. It can also be used negatively — as wrath — against the enemies of Christianity. Embedded, therefore, in this passage are two qualities of God, glory and power. The power of God will be used in the bowls of wrath that will be spilled out upon the persecutors of Christianity as chapter 16 now discloses.

Reflection

1. The hymns of Revelation have inspired many Christian composers. How do Christian hymns help me with my faith?
2. Scriptural "glory" refers to the religious experience of God's presence. What experiences of "glory" have I known in my life?
3. How are the Eucharistic tabernacles in our parish churches similar to the Ark of the Covenant? How are they different?
4. What are my favorite hymns? What do I like most about them?
5. What is the most impressive church I have ever seen? What moved me about it?
6. How can I appreciate the importance of the temple for the people of the Jewish Covenant?
7. The most sacred part of the temple was the Holy of Holies. What is the most sacred part of my parish church? Why?
8. What are three manifestations in nature that make me think of the glory of God?

9. How does my religion help me preserve a sense of the sacred in a secular culture?
10. What is there about my own body and soul that I consider sacred no matter what the culture tries to make me think?

Prayer

Eucharistic Jesus, your Real Presence is in the tabernacle of my parish church. I promise to visit you there more often. I will come and look at you and you will look at me. In that communion of love, I pray you will increase my faith and strengthen me for the daily struggle to witness you more truly and bring your affection to others.

16 The Bowls of God's Wrath

The seven bowls of wrath are very similar to the terrors that accompanied the seven seals and the seven trumpets. They are also comparable to the ten plagues of Egypt described in Exodus 7-12. Only four of the Egyptian plagues appear here: The waters becoming blood, the sores on the body, the thunder and hail, the darkness. John does not use ten plagues because his judgment imagery is always in terms of sevens. The bowls of wrath smite the four traditional elements that compose the world — earth, air, fire, and water. This destruction of the natural world prepares for God's creation of a new heaven and a new earth (see 21:1). The following chart gives you a chance to see how closely these are connected. I have changed the order to show where bowls and plagues match.

Plagues of Egypt	Bowls of Wrath
1. Water turned to blood (Exodus 7:20-25)	1. Sea becomes like blood of dead man (16:3)
	2. Rivers and Fountains become blood. (16:4)
2. Boils and Sores (9:8-11)	3. Ulcerous sores (16:2)
3. Thunder and Hail (9:22-26)	4. Thunder, Hail (16:2)
4. Darkness (10:21-23)	5. Darkness (16:10)
5. The frogs (8:5-14)	6. Sun scorches (16:8)
6. The lice (8:16-18	7. Dry Euphrates (16:12)
7. The flies (8:20-24)	
8. The cattle (9:3-6)	
9. Locusts (10:12-19)	
10. Slay first-born (12:29-30)	

The Flaw of the Fundamentalist Interpretation

There is little doubt that John envisioned these bowls of wrath as meant for the Roman empire. At the same time his prophecies have a continual relevance for the history of the church. Evil is self-destructive at both a personal and social level. Sinful individuals incur the outcome of their behavior. Corrupt nations slide into the morass of their own decadence. God's judgment simply confirms what people and nations already have done to themselves. This happened to a decadent Roman Empire. It was repeated in the "evil empire" of the Communist Soviet Union in our own day. Church history has numerous examples of such occurrences.

Fundamentalist Christians look at the woes of the seven seals, seven trumpets, and seven bowls of wrath in Revelation 6-16 and call them "tribulations." There is no doubt that such tribulations have happened again and again in church history. Plagues, wars, earthquakes, diseases, floods, and social breakdowns have occurred over and over. Sometimes they are related to persecutors of the church and sometimes not.

The question raised by Fundamentalist Christians is, "Will the tribulations be part of the story of the end of the world?" Christ's Last Judgment sermons indicate that there will be catastrophes related to the end of the world and his second coming. But he speaks of that in a general way. He does not name the number of woes, nor the number of years these might last. Nor does he foretell the exact date of such sorrows.

Fundamentalist Christians preach a millenarian view of the end of the world. Their overall view is that there will be four steps marking the end of time: (1) A "rapture" of the just into union with Jesus Christ; (2) Seven years of tribulations for the wicked on earth; (3) A thousand-year reign of the kingdom of God on earth; (4) Finally, the Second Coming of Christ and the end of the world. On the question of the tribulations, some Fundamentalists see these happening just after the rapture and before the thousand-year reign. Others claim the tribulations (including Armageddon) will come after the thousand-year reign just before the Second Coming.

I will deal with this millenarian interpretation of Scripture more extensively in chapter 20 of this book. You could read it right now if you wish. Here I just want to focus on the matter of the tribulations. The fatal flaw of the Fundamentalists' interpretation is a too literal understanding of the texts and a hunger to tie it to predicted dates. This causes them to look for signs of the times, especially certain political developments as well as worldwide examples of social turmoil and upset as presumably clear examples of the coming end of the world. This is especially true when they are looking for literal examples of the "tribulations."

Since there are always wars and rumors of wars, always terrible natural catastrophes, always unfortunate examples of moral decay, it is not hard to identify tribulations. The problem for the interpreter is that the tribulations of one's own times may or may not be signs of the end. We simply do not know. In the Middle Ages, when the Black Plague ravaged Europe like germ warfare, the results were so horrible and depressing that millions believed the end of the world was coming. Yet that did not occur.

The important issue for us is not wasting our energies on whether or not we can foretell history's end, but whether we are ready to meet God at any moment of our lives. Tragedies, disasters, personal afflictions are invitations to personal and moral renewal and conversion. Tribulations should call each of us to hear the call to holiness and spirituality. It does not matter whether these are the final tribulations or just another round of this world's typical woes. What does matter is the state of our personal lives, our moral integrity, and our capacity to love God, others, and self.

Empires rise and fall. Cultures live and die. The cycle of birth, ascendancy, decline and death mark nature, history, and each human person. There is nothing new about it. What is to be gained by trying to be a predictor of the end of the world? What kind of need is satisfied? In my opinion, very little indeed. Moreover, when this tactic is used for political purposes, such as supporting certain balances of military power in the Middle East, then such interpretations become mischievous and could be harmful to people's lives. The principal value of tribulations is their spiritual usefulness in our ongoing faith conversions, not some imagined tool for prophesying the end of time. John provides the best advice,

"Blessed is the one who watches" (verse 15). Not watching for the curtain to come down, but one's conscience and one's spiritual growth.

Armageddon

"They then assembled the kings in the place that is named Armageddon" (verse 16). Armageddon most likely refers to the mount of Megiddo in northern Palestine. The hill of Megiddo is located near the Mediterranean sea. Megiddo borders a broad valley where many battles have been fought. Today is it a scene of fruitful farms. It is about fifteen miles wide and twenty miles long. This area has also been called the Plain of Esdraelon.

Fundamentalists see this as the very place where the final war of the world will be fought. It is clearly too small for the imagined millions who will fight, but it will be the marshalling place for the opposing armies. The war will be fought, so they say, between the Mediterranean sea and the Euphrates river. These armies will be locked in combat in Jerusalem itself on the very day of the Second Coming. Such a battle will coincide with the establishing of a "world government." The present talk about a "new world order" gives Fundamentalists fresh ammunition for foreseeing the world government.

Demons will inflame the warriors. Demonic spirits "went out to the kings of the whole world to assemble them for the battle on the great day of God the almighty" (verse 14). If there is a world government why is there such a big war? Presumably the answer is a civil war in which rival factions struggle for world supremacy. The evil world compounds its evil. Fundamentalists contend that this battle at Armageddon will last several months, after which will be the Second Coming of Jesus. The Lord will arrive with his armies and overcome the soldiers of the demonic spirits.

To create this scenario takes a good deal of skipping around the texts of Scripture to make it all fit. The basic assumption is that the books of Ezekiel, Daniel, Christ's Last Judgment sermons, certain texts in the epistles, and the Book of Revelation itself are like a great crossword puzzle, a divine secret code that needs to be unraveled and reordered to describe the last days.

But scriptural scholarship calls us to read each book in the context of its times, the intentions of the authors, the purposes of the books, the state of the people to whom the words were addressed. Biblical scholars also operate within the faith of the church and the guidance of its Magisterium. The Fundamentalist stitching together of texts from all over the Bible to prove a point is not helpful and is contrary to the spirit and reality of the texts. No question but that Fundamentalist Christians have a deep and admirable faith in Jesus Christ. They are committed to moral values and strive to live the Gospel with considerable energy. But their scholarship is underdeveloped. Their principles for biblical interpretation are too literalist. They seem unaware of the symbolic uses of Scripture.

Blessed Is the One Who Watches

All of the challenging scenes in the book of revelation are designed to produce Christian alertness. These are wake-up calls to the church and to all her members. Religion's greatest problem is the routine into which its members can lapse. It is not so much that Christians are bad, but rather they have a tendency to sloth. Laziness threatens the church. This spiritual apathy reduces beliefs to pat formulas, worship to ritualism, morality to minimal efforts at keeping the rules and church membership to a passive, amiable, and non-enthusiastic participation.

This is why God always sends prophets to the church. Prophets comfort the afflicted. They also afflict the comfortable. Now John's Revelation is a book of prophecies. John assumes the role of a prophet for the church. Regrettably, some people regard the prophecies as intriguing clues to figure out how and when the world will end. They make Revelation into a religious hobby. Their pleasure comes from unraveling the images and "breaking the code." Looking at the book this way distracts them from the true purpose of the prophecies, which is to call Christians to wake up and put their lives in order, whether the world is ending or not.

John wants to shake us up, to pull us out of our religious lethargy, to be on the watch for what is corrupting our lives. "Blessed is the one who watches" (verse 15). It is too easy to have fun with the texts as though they were a secret code. It is far harder to see them as a public code, the law of God calling us to renewal. Yet that is the hard message of Revelation. Actually, responding to it this way is much more humanly satisfying — and spiritually valuable.

Reflection

1. A "bowl of wrath" symbolizes God's power and judgment. What examples of God's judgment can I share with others?
2. How would I respond to a Fundamentalist who wanted to convince me the world will end on such or such a date?
3. Suppose I were to experience all the tribulations described in the seven seals/trumpets/bowls of wrath. What would I think?
4. What is the scriptural purpose of the tribulations? What impact should they have on me?
5. How would religious sloth or laziness affect my moral and spiritual life?
6. Why is faith vigilance so important?
7. Why is scriptural scholarship and the guidance of the church's Magisterium so important for interpreting Revelation?
8. Why is the "new world order" not necessarily a sign of the end of the world?
9. Instead of interpreting Scripture as a giant crossword puzzle, what should we really do?
10. Why do prophets both afflict the comfortable and comfort the afflicted?

Prayer

Lord Jesus, by your glory you give me an experience of your presence. By your power you enable my spiritual growth. By your judgment you remind me of the logical outcome of my behavior on my destiny. I praise your glory, power and judgment. I sing of your salvation and ask for a greater openness to its benefits for me. Come to me, Lord Jesus. Come soon with all your love.

17 Who Is the Scarlet Woman?

Never Forget the Real Purpose of This Book

The spectacular language and tumbling symbols of Revelation tend to distract us from what is being said. This tempts us to look at the trees and forget the forest. This final section of Revelation so vividly describes a prostitute that the image distracts from its purpose. Some prim religious people use these passages as permission to dwell on seamy applications. After all, Scripture paints for us the picture of a scarlet woman. Should we not amplify it to expand the lurid implications of the image? No, we should not. Scripture calls us to concentrate on the core message of Revelation.

Recall again what this book teaches us. The church has left Judaism behind. Newly born by the Spirit at Pentecost, the church must walk through the desert of history and grow to maturity in Jesus Christ. Exodus taught that Israel encountered many chastening experiences that purified her faith and molded her into the first people of God. Revelation imparts the same truth. The infant church has marched into the desert of history and confronts a pagan persecution which appears to threaten her very existence. Providence and history are shaping the church into the new and final people of God.

The whole Bible has unfolded God's plan for us. Scripture reveals a cycle of sin, purification, and salvation, repeated again and again. In the Old Testament God raised up prophets to remind God's people of this rhythm of religious life and to point them toward a promise of a savior who would be the ultimate redeemer. This event occurred in the birth, life, death, and resurrection of the Son of God and son of Mary, Jesus Christ our Lord.

But the cycle of God's plan continues. The Book of Revelation makes this abundantly clear. Jesus is not the end of history. He is the beginning of new age and a new form of the cycle of God's plan for his people. The disclosure of the Word of God in the Old Testament experience, written in the revealed word, achieved perfect fulfillment in the Incarnation of Jesus Christ. The story is not over. What happened in Jesus continues in the church, the sacraments, and the Christian witness of God's new people.

Revelation has been born as a person — Jesus. It must grow and be applied in the lives of the Christian people. Jesus has died and risen from the dead. He has sent his Spirit to us so that he may die and rise in each one of us. The coming of the Lamb, slain and triumphant, is not something that will only happen at the end of time. The Lamb seeks to be spiritually slain and triumphant in each of our lives because that is how we are personally redeemed and how the world itself is saved.

I have said it often enough before, but must repeat it here: Revelation is not an "ultra-secret" or a mysterious code that outlines the details of the end of the world. Seen this way, an interpreter tries to match its imagery with political events and natural disasters and then create a scenario for the end of time. This trivializes the intention of Revelation. I have pointed out that the book speaks at three levels: (1) The experience of the infant church; (2) The course of Christian history; (3) The end of time.

In other words, Revelation is a divine guidebook, relevant to every period of Christian history. It tells every new generation of Christians how to live in the desert of history with the cycle of sin, purification, and redemption. New life constantly emerges from the crucible of pain and persecution in every age. The Spirit applies the power of Christ's salvation to every person who has come to Jesus in faith, becomes actively involved in the church and sacraments and witnesses courage and responsibility in the world.

Revelation stands between the two comings of Jesus. Its message fosters consolation to a church that reaches its glory through suffering. It stimulates hope to believers sometimes daunted by their own personal sufferings and the agonies imposed by ruthless leaders in society and government. Of all the books of the Bible, Revelation presents the most powerful encouragement to us to wait with patience the fulfillment of God's merciful plan for us. Certainly, it bids us look back to the early Christian community and forward to the Last Judgment. Above all it says, "Look at your present situation."

The Whore of Babylon (17:1-18)

Two of the most striking images in Revelation focus on women. Chapter 12 portrays the dramatic woman of Creation. She wears the cosmic jewelry of sun and stars and stands on the moon, the symbol of night and its evil. She keeps evil under her heel. The best interpretation of this dazzling woman is Mary, the mother of God. Pregnant with Jesus, she is the "Theotokos," the God-bearer. Mary is the mother of the savior. She symbolizes the church which is the efficacious community of salvation through its sacraments and its call to holiness.

In this chapter we see a different woman. She is the whore of Babylon — a code word both for imperial Rome and all pagan nations that persecute the church. Just as Mary symbolizes the church of love, mercy, and hope, the whore symbolizes the kingdoms of hatred, harshness, and despair. She is at once the kept woman of these empires as well as the empires themselves.

John unsparingly describes her evil traits. She wears the scarlet color of her trade. She sits on a scarlet beast. She is the embodiment of the beast we have already seen as (1) the dragon — an enlargement of Eden's serpent; (2) the beast from the sea — the leviathan; (3) the beast from the land — the behemoth, also called the Antichrist. Whereas Mary, the woman of the Apocalypse, is different from the dragon, that is, intrinsically different from the incarnation of evil, this woman is essentially identified with evil. Blasphemous names appear on her head. She holds aloft a gold cup filled with the abominable and sordid deeds of her harlotry. She was "drunk with the blood of the holy ones and on the blood of the witnesses to Jesus" (verse 6).

Another Look at the Antichrist

Lest we get too carried away with a woman-symbol of evil, we should pause a moment and look at a male image of evil. In his second letter to the Thessalonians, Paul speaks of the Antichrist as a man of lawlessness. The sign of presence of the Antichrist is a widespread experience of lawlessness. In passing I might note that the prevalence of disrespect for laws and rules, both in our society and the church, our cultural lawlessness, is a sign of the success of a present-day Antichrist.

I am not saying this is the definitive Antichrist who will be present at the end of time, but one more example of the numerous Antichrists who have existed throughout history. Our current repudiation of standards, rules, and laws (both civil and divine) seems to me to fit Paul's description of how the Antichrist works in a given period of history.

Paul goes on to say that "the lawless one will be revealed, whom the Lord [Jesus] will kill with the breath of his mouth and render powerless by the manifestation of his coming" (II Thes. 2:8). In other words, Scripture uses both a male and a female to speak of the Antichrist. This moral impartiality reminds us that both genders are equally capable of the worst sinfulness and both can be invoked as symbols of evil. I think John chose a female for his book because he wanted to contrast her with the Woman of Grace whose Son defeats the dragon.

The Whore/Beast as Politician

Whereas Paul identifies the Antichrist in general terms as some real, concrete man who fosters rebellion against the laws, customs, and rules of society and the church, John names the Antichrist as a political ruler. Just as our Creed remembers the craven politician, Pontius Pilate, as the one who ordered the death of Christ, so John connects the Antichrist with political rulers who persecuted the Body of Christ, the church. He could have been referring to Nero, or to the Nero-like Domitian.

During the Reformation, Calvin and Luther called the pope the

Antichrist and the whore of Babylon. Popes of the time were political rulers of the papal states, as well as spiritual leaders of the church. The sermons of Luther and Calvin and other reformers built luxuriant attacks against the popes by using the imagery found in this seventeenth chapter of Revelation.

In our own time, militant anti-Catholic, Fundamentalist preachers entertain their congregations with lurid descriptions of the modern popes in very much the same language. Even within the Catholic Church, factions opposed to the popes for their positions on abortion, homosexuality, and the ordination of women come close to using this chapter for their fulminations. Their overheated accusations are embarrassing, unbefitting, and just plain wrong. Polemic has replaced civilized discourse. Rebellion has overshadowed obedience. Obviously chapter 17 fascinates some modern readers looking for language to harass their enemies. Satan knows how to turn Christians against one another.

Battle of Beast and Lamb

The remainder of chapter 17 reiterates the story of the conflict of good and evil already outlined in various ways in other chapters. The difference here is that the enemy is larger than just Rome. The beast is still Rome, of course. "The seven heads (of the beast) represent the seven hills upon which the woman sits" (verse 9). The use of "seven hills" is a clear allusion to Rome. But in addition there are ten kings in league with Rome and joining in the attack on the church. These are probably the client states of the East who follow Rome's lead in this suppression of Christianity. John gives us his interpretations of the various figures, the beast, the woman, and the horns. It is consistent with what we have been seeing all along in this book.

As always, we must repeatedly ask, "Where does all this leave us?" What are we to do with the image of the scarlet woman so plainly thrown into the well of our awareness by this chapter? What has all this to do with our lives? I suggest the following direction that is based on our general approach to God's Word and our daily lives.

The Split-Level Human and God's Word

One of the reasons why we find it hard to read Scripture is our western, mental outlook. We have been trained to put a wall between our heads and our hearts. Our minds and wills inhabit two different worlds. We have become split-level humans. We expect our heads to explain life with logic and clarity. We turn to our hearts for "reasons" that have nothing to do with reason. This is why we can oppose compassion and truth. We assume that the compassion of our hearts should be so attractive and appealing that we should pay no attention to our minds that tell us we are wrongheaded in a compassion that denies moral truth.

This approach destroys the natural interaction of mind and heart, of thought and will power. The wall prevents the interplay. The result is that our minds have no influence on emotions. And our wills do not influence our thoughts. This causes moral schizophrenia. The mind says it is wrong. The heart says it is right. This disconnects faith from Christian behavior. What everyone is doing becomes the norm for behavior. Truth is not in the mind but in action. Experience is the arbiter of truth, not the workings of the mind.

This is why polls become so deadly when applied to Christian teachings. The assumption is that if most Catholics behave contrary to some faith teaching of Scripture and the church, then something should be done to change the teaching. But the Bible would say in such a case, "Don't change the teaching. Change the behavior."

Because our minds and hearts are free-floating worlds, disconnected from each other, it becomes very difficult to defend the truth of the Bible and the Magisterium of the church. The strangeness of Revelation would not seem nearly so odd if our hearts and minds were connected to each other. We should have an inner order: emotions subject to will, will obedient to mind, mind obedient to God.

Biblical people did not think as we do. They did not divide their inner life into sealed chambers. Their inner life was porous, mind-heart-emotions all affecting one another. Theirs was a healthier inner life, rich with the interplay of imagination, thinking, feeling, and deciding. Their ideas were not cold abstractions, but warmed with imagination and feeling.

Their wills were more than matters of choice, disengaged from the thinking process and the role of the light of truth. The biblical will was normally pro-life, not pro-choice. We see what goes wrong when the will acts too independently in Genesis. The opening chapters of Genesis describe Adam and Eve leaving their brains at the door and putting all their hopes on choice alone, on what we subsequently called their rebellious wills.

Biblical people's passions and feelings were loud and clear, but part of the mosaic of mind and heart — and body for that matter. Theirs was a holistic outlook, far different from our split-level mentalities.

Of course this did not prevent them from sinning, but it did allow them to be honest enough to say so. And when a person or nation denied its sinfulness, the prophets were there to tell them about hard hearts and stiff necks.

How to Restore Unity

(1) *Reaffirm the conviction that truth can be known.* Our culture thrives on opinions. So widespread has this become that everyone is led to believe there are only changeable opinions and no truth to be found. We are told to prize pluralism because we are such a diverse culture. This is a half-truth. We should honor our differences. We should also revere our unity. That is why multiformity is a better ideal than pluralism. Multiformity implies there is truth and unity amid many diverse expressions.

The Book of Revelation has basically one truth to teach, namely, that the church comes to glory through suffering, just as Jesus came to Resurrection through the cross. Revelation uses the principle of multiformity to teach this one truth. Its vast album of different images — seals, trumpets, bowls of wrath, the Lamb, the woman clothed with the sun, the heavenly choirs — form a mosaic that reveals a basic unity and truth. When we reaffirm that conviction the truth can be known, then we make an act of support for our minds, our brains, and their ability to know truth.

(2) *Place the will at the service of truth and God.* There is no Christianity without the obedience of faith. Obedience is an honest submission of the will to truth and to God. When our wills are

oriented to obedience, then our behavior acts out the vision of truth and the will of God. A will disconnected from the mind, truth, and God does its own thing. A will united to intelligence, reality, and the love of God does what is best for human development, the harmony of the human community, and the honor of God. The harmony of will and mind cures the split-level human.

(3) *Rein in the passions and emotions.* Feelings are like March wind. They blow where they want. Feelings are full of energy, but they are blind. They need direction from the mind and will. Deep feelings can be tremendous servants of faith and love. They can also be destructive of Christian living. It all depends on whether they are directed by faith or left to wander on their own. They will either master us or be mastered by us. There is no in-between. Put passions and emotions in God's service.

When we connect mind, will, and emotions in a harmonious unity we will begin to identify with the mind-set of the biblical mentality. We will also begin to see more clearly the point of Revelation.

Reflection

1. In the light of my study and prayer up to this point, what would I say is the purpose of the Book of Revelation?
2. Why is it not a good idea to see Revelation as a book that only talks about the end of the world?
3. What lesson can I draw from Paul's "man of lawlessness" and John's "whore of Babylon"?
4. Why do some emotional preachers love to use the imagery of whore of Babylon in their sermons?
5. How would I respond to a Fundamentalist who calls the pope the whore of Babylon?
6. If an Antichrist is a "man of lawlessness," what would be the evidence for that in our own culture?
7. In what ways do I experience myself as a "split-level" person as described in this chapter?
8. Why is the harmony of my mind, will, and emotions important for understanding Scripture?

9. How has the persecution of the church been a positive experience for the Body of Christ?
10. How does my own pain affect my faith life?

Prayer

Lord of history, you have overthrown persecutors of true believers time and again throughout the Christian era. The suffering has purified the church and served as the seed of new and stronger faith. In our own day believers still suffer for their faith in China, Burma, Vietnam, and in some Moslem countries. May they be strengthened and comforted by you. I praise you, my Lord and God.

18 The Twilight of the Gods

The Last Judgment

Behind the altar of the Sistine Chapel is Michelangelo's fresco of the Last Judgment. It fills up the entire wall with the majesty of the end of time. Fifty-five feet high. Forty feet wide. On that vast wall, Michelangelo painted three hundred men, women, children, angels, saints, and demons. He catches each human being at a moment of profound self-appraisal. All evasions and self-deceptions have vanished. All the people are shown as responsible for their behavior on earth. Every man, woman, and child stands out in pure clarity, superbly human, framed by the crisp air about each figure.

This rousing crowd of characters surround Christ. Groups of bodies rise upward on one side and descend on the other. The yawning cave of hell, the burial ground of eternity, occupies the bottom of the fresco. Jesus dominates the middle. Michelangelo loved to capture a figure at a moment of truth, of epochal decision. Out of the agony of this decision making came the vision of truth. Hence the spark that depicts God at the moment of creating Adam, of David just before the battle with Goliath, of Moses ascending Sinai. These moments breathe truth.

Jesus Christ explodes on the scene with a sudden burst of force, light, and firmness. All the peoples of history flow toward him with awe. The artist drew back the right leg of Christ, catching him in moving forward to regain balance, placing him in the tension this would cause. While Jesus indeed is the compassionate God, he also has the serious business of justice. He embodies awesomeness.

Next to Jesus is Mary. She is a young, strong, life-giving woman. At the same time she radiates the glory of heaven. She turns her face away from the judgment against unrepentant sinners. As Mother of Mercy she had always prayed for the salvation of souls.

She had stretched out her hand to sinners to lead them toward conversion. It is now too painful for her to see what self-destruction unrepentant sinners had brought upon themselves.

We see before us a naked humanity being held accountable for how they lived their lives on earth. Even the just ones holding the signs of their good lives seem stunned by the appearance of the Lord of history. That moment of uneasiness, even for the just, reminds us that salvation is finally a gift of God to those who have trusted and believed in him. The whole scene erupts like a clap of thunder and rushes into levels of our awareness we like to hide from ourselves. We prefer sound-bites of truth. Michelangelo's Last Judgment is a cyclone of revelation. It puts fresh meaning back into the word, "unforgettable."

Up to this point our meditations have dwelt on the three applications of Revelation. However, we have looked mainly on the historical background of the book and some contemporary applications. I believe it is now time to concentrate on its relevance to the actual end of time. That is the reason for introducing this chapter with a description of Michelangelo's Last Judgment. Chapters 18-22 serve the purpose of a closing reflection on the end of the world.

Some say there are only two certainties in life: death and taxes. Revelation adds a third certainty — judgment against evil persons and nations and judgment in favor of the just. In its description of the fall of Babylon, chapter 18 spells out the judgment of God against human sinfulness. It speaks of the justice of God. The final chapters of revelation will tell us of the merciful judgment of God toward repentant sinners whose contrition opened them to the loving forgiveness of God.

The Last Judgment will reveal both the justice and mercy of God. The condemnation of the wicked exposes the justice of God. The salvation of the just discloses Christ's mercy. The exaltation of the just clearly manifests divine love. The Last Judgment will also tell us of the wisdom of God. While on earth we struggled to make sense out of suffering. We wept at the prosperity of the wicked and mourned the oppression of the just. We failed to understand the death of the young and the early departure of the saints, while the tyrants seemed to live far too long. At the Last Judgment, these mysteries will be solved, for at last we will see how the plan of God really worked out in human life.

Jesus Christ will come to judge the living and the dead. His first coming at Bethlehem was in poverty and humility. The Savior allowed people to cause him pain and kill him. But at the Second Coming Jesus will appear with power and glory. As the Son of God he will have the right to judge all peoples. As the son of Mary, he became the Savior. So, even in his humanity, Jesus will be a judge. He will have the power to distinguish those who have been saved by his passion and Resurrection from those who rejected it. When this judgment is finished, the present world will truly end and only the world to come will exist.

The Twilight of the Gods (18:1-10)

German mythology, especially as captured in the music of Richard Wagner, portrays the arrogance of the gods and their demise. This is called the twilight of the gods. The fall of the Roman Empire, the collapse of the Third Reich, and the breakup of Soviet Communism are dramatic historical examples of this mythological outcome of human pride and sinfulness.

These bold samples of the suicide of nations and cultures apply to individual, unrepentant sinners. Each individual must account for personal destiny. What happens to evil nations occurs to evil persons. God's justice not only applies to countries, it also affects individuals. The value of meditating on the Fall of Babylon in chapter 18 is that it describes the result of the corruption of a human soul as well as a national culture. The twilight of the gods includes you and me. We are not really dealing with a German myth, but with the teachings of the revealed Word of God.

"Fallen, fallen is Babylon the great" (verse 2). Historically, John is talking about the eventual fall of Rome. Prophetically, he is telling us about the Last Judgment. Here is the end of time, the final outcome of the seven seals, the seven trumpets, and the seven bowls of wrath. God's justice is ultimately revealed. Not only is Rome held to accountability, but all the sinful nations of history. "For all the nations have drunk the wine of her licentious passion" (verse 3).

Their sins are piled up to the sky. God remembers all their evil. The totality of the prophecies in the seals, trumpets, and bowls of wrath come crashing down on them. The kings who had intercourse with Babylon will try to run away from her. Actually, they will attempt to escape their own accountability, but will not be allowed to do so. This will be not just the twilight of a god, but of the gods — more accurately, the godless. This will be equally true of each person who has refused the grace, love, and forgiveness of God.

The Tears of the Selfish Rich (18:11-24)

"The merchants who . . . grew rich from her, will cry out . . . 'In one hour this great wealth has been ruined' " (verses 15,17). Their tears are purely selfish. They had no love of Rome. They only loved the money they could make from sales and trade. They cooperated with evil and will suffer the same judgment. Not only is their wealth ruined, but their souls as well. John lists twenty-five products which the merchants sold to gain wealth. See verses 12-13.

The Romans had a passion for silver. In Spain, thousands worked the silver mines to satisfy the tables of rich Romans. They ate from sterling silver dishes, fought with swords whose hilts were silver, gazed on their faces in silver mounted mirrors. One Roman general carried with him 12,000 pounds of silver dishes on his campaigns. They also bought up diamonds, pearls, purple silk, spices, cinnamon, myrrh, and articles made of ivory, walnut, bronze, and marble. Also "slaves, that is, human beings" (verse 13). "Use your slaves like the limbs of your body," says a Roman writer, "each for its own end." For some slaves their only job was to help the rich remember their names, when to eat, and when to retire. Some slaves were beautiful boys and young men, others beautiful girls and young women — purchased for obvious reasons.

John leaves little to our imagination when finally exposing the corruption of sin. The tears of the selfish merchants are of the same order as the groans of the disappointed kings. They had tied their human destinies to a decadent harlot. Their political alliances and business agreements with the "whore of Babylon" made them as corrupt as their client.

The Five Results of the Millstone of Selfishness

"A mighty angel picked up a stone like a huge millstone and threw it into the sea and said, 'With such force will Babylon . . . be thrown down and will never be found again' " (verse 21). An angel threw a millstone into the sea to swamp them all. They had degraded thousands of human beings to support their vanity and pride. Nothing is left but silence. John lists five outcomes of their behavior.

1. *The music stopped* (verse 22a). Generally music is associated with joy, though it also accompanies mourning. Here the author means that happiness has vanished from the lives of these people. They had imagined that constant joy could be found in power, wealth, and self-gratification. They used power to make slaves of millions. They spent money to surround themselves with things. They made self-indulgence a philosophy. It was as though each of them said, "I am what I control. I am what I own. I am what gives me pleasure." Their search for identity in pure selfishness finally caused the music to stop. Lasting happiness can only be found in serving others, not dominating them. Constant joy comes from freedom from things, not grasping them. True contentment derives from making others feel good, not from stroking oneself. For the damned at the Judgment, the message will be, "No melodies will ever be heard in you again" (verse 22a).

2. *Productivity ceased* (verse 22b). The monks of the Middle Ages had a wise saying that applies here: "Diligence begets abundance. Abundance begets laxity. Laxity begets decadence." When the Roman Empire was ascendant it possessed the discipline and virtues that made it prosperous. But with abundance it grew soft. That is when it sought power for its own sake, wealth as an end in itself, and self-gratification as the only goal in life. Fat and lax, the empire sank into decadence. Productivity ceased. "No craftsmen in any trade will ever be found in you again" (verse 22b). Economic collapse has happened again and again to nations, empires, and families who have lost the discipline and virtues that made them prosper. History also shows that religious faith and spirituality are the power behind the moral strength that makes cultures and families grow. When that disappears the road to decline sets in.

3. *Family life disintegrated.* "No sound of the millstone will ever be heard in you again" (verse 22c). Families disappear. John uses the symbol of the millstone to make this point. Grinding corn and wheat was done at home. Families had two heavy circular stones (millstones), one on top of the other. Wheat or corn was put through a hole in the upper stone and was ground as it fell between the revolving stones. The sound of a millstone was a familiar one in any household. Now it will never be heard again. More to the point, the happy noise of family life has gone. When the empire, the nation, and the culture cease to support family values, there will be no family. The destruction of the family is suicide for the nation. When there is a strong family then a sense of God and the reality of the sacred is present. A feeling for God and reverence for the sacred are absolutely necessary for the powerful virtues that build a culture and a society. When the nation betrays family values and even enacts laws to undermine them, then the nation has no future. The sound of the millstone stops.

4. *The lights went out.* On the eve of World War II, it was said, "The lights have gone out all over Europe." That was literally true because of the bombings which called for blackouts every night. It was symbolically true because the judgment descended on the free nations that failed to stand up against the intimidation of the Nazi threats. They lacked the moral fiber to restrain the lust of the dictators. Night descended on Europe. The tragic image is useful because it gives us a contemporary look at what we can expect at the end of time. Immorality will cause the light of all that civilization tried to accomplish to die out. Sinfulness causes darkness. Jesus said he was the light. Those who follow him walk in the light. Those who do not become his disciples will walk in the dark. Light stands for truth in the mind and virtue in action. Those who choose lies for their minds and vice for their behavior have picked darkness as their habitat. "No light from a lamp will ever be seen in you again" (verse 23a).

5. *The weddings stopped.* Marriage is necessary for the continuation of the race, the culture, and the family. In Roman times the average life-span was 30-35 years. Infant mortality rates were high. Only 4 men in 100 lived beyond the age of 50 — and fewer

women because so many died in childbirth. A family was very concerned about the preservation of its wealth and future name. The Roman government expected women to have at least five children. The cemeteries near their towns were vivid reminders of the shortness of life and the need to marry and have children. They realized how tenuous was their hold on life and its continuity and stability. This is why the corruption of the culture and the empire was so devastating. It was hard enough to keep things going when discipline and virtue prevailed. It was impossible when these essentials failed. "No voices of bride and groom will ever be heard in you again" (verse 23b).

Why did all this happen? Greed. "Because your merchants were the great ones of the world, all nations were led astray by your magic potion" (verse 23c). Of the seven capital sins, greed is the worst. Paul said as much in his letter to Timothy. "The love of money is the root of all evils, and some people in their desire for it have strayed from the faith and pierced themselves with many pains" (I Tm. 6:10).

Money is not the cause of evil. It is the greed for it that produces evil. The "love of money" is the problem. John calls it a "magic potion." In other words it is a drug that makes its seekers succumb to its addiction. Should we be surprised that in our own day, with its shameful examples of greed and obsession with wealth, that literal drug addiction is at an all-time high? Addiction to money has led to addiction with drugs. The self-destruction that avarice causes goes far beyond what the "merchants" want for themselves. It affects all of society and culture — and the family itself.

John says that at the judgment there will be an ominous silence in the world. Joy will cease. Productivity will vanish. Family life will die. Darkness will prevail. Bride and bridegroom will no longer toast each other. Why? Because the love of money generates all these evils. The magic potion will drug the world into self-annihilation. Jesus teaches there are only two gods, money and Our Father in heaven. We cannot serve both of them. We must choose. Jesus wants us to choose life, love, and salvation — given us by the true God of heaven. Otherwise we will opt for death, hatred, damnation, given to us by the false god of the love of money.

"Fallen, fallen is Babylon the great" (verse 2). As we look at our own avaricious culture, we might say, "Fallen, fallen is western culture," unless we repent. There are and have been intermediate judgments before the last one. These are dress rehearsals. It would be a pity to let that happen to us in our day. Why? Because we know what can be done to stop it. We have the medicine of truth for the disease of our times. Is there a doctor in the house?

Reflection

1. If I were to describe the Last Judgment in my own words, what would I say?
2. Why is it important to note that the Last Judgment will show both the justice and the mercy of God?
3. How will the Last Judgment help us to see God's wisdom in relation to the sorrows and sufferings of this life?
4. Why is John's description of the fall of Babylon important for me personally?
5. For the damned, there will be no more joy. The music will stop. What is the main cause of the loss of human happiness?
6. Economic productivity declines in corrupt cultures. How might this principle apply to our own culture?
7. What reasons do I see for the erosion of family values in our society?
8. How can married people and their families preserve the sense of the sacred and faith in God?
9. Why is the "love of money" the real root of all evil?
10. What connection could I draw between obsession with money and addiction to drugs?

Prayer

Just and merciful judge, you will come to judge the living and the dead. In your justice you will confirm the wickedness of evil people and send them to hell. In your mercy you will confirm the faith and obedience of good people and bring them to heaven. In your wisdom you will reveal how your plan makes sense out of suffering. I adore you, my Lord. I love you and pray for the conversion of all.

19 The Wedding Feast of the Lamb

The Hallelujah Chorus (19:1-10)

From the moment we heard the approaching hoofbeats of the four horsemen of the Apocalypse in chapter 6 until now, we have been flooded with images of plagues, wars, tears, death, and destruction — all culminating in the fall of Babylon in chapter 18. At the same time, hints and signs of hope kept up our spirits, above all with the sign of the great woman in the sky, crowned with stars and clothed with the sun, holding evil under her feet and pregnant with the Redeemer who will slay the dragon, overcome the behemoth, and defeat the Antichrist.

In these last four chapters the mighty duel between good and evil comes to an end. Jesus Christ, Lord of lords and King of kings, has won the battle against sin and death. He has triumphed over evil empires that persecuted believers and avaricious people who dehumanized millions to achieve their goals.

This already occurred in his death and resurrection. But it needed to be realized and experienced in subsequent history. Christ's victory is applied to all those who surrender to him in faith and obedience from his first coming in Galilee to his final coming at the end of time. At a deeper level, Christ's salvation is experienced by all the souls of the just from the beginning of time to its end.

The Praise Songs of the Redeemed

The best way to imagine the opening of chapter 19 is to envision a great stage with an enormous choir singing rapturous praises to God for the absolute victory over evil. "Alleluia! Salvation, glory, and might belong to our God. . . . Let us rejoice and be glad and give him glory" (verses 1,7). Thousands of verses in the Bible tell the dreary story of human sinfulness. Happily, thousands more contain a tapestry of praise songs gratefully adoring God for the gift of salvation. This is especially clear in the psalms and in the hymns of Revelation.

"Sing to the Lord a new song. . . . Sing to the Lord, bless his name, announce his salvation day after day" (Ps. 96:1-2). What virtue dominates these full-throated acclamations of God? Love, and love alone. The redeemed recognize God's magnificent love and boisterously respond with countless love songs. This music of joy is a melody of love.

Saint Augustine puts it this way. "Anyone who has learned to love the new life has learned to sing a new song. . . . We cannot love unless someone has loved us first. The source of our love for God can only be found in the fact that God loved us first. This love is not something we generate ourselves. It comes to us through the Holy Spirit who has been given to us. God offers us a short route to the possession of himself. God cries out: 'Love me and you will have me, for you would be unable to love me if you did not already possess me' " (*Sermon 34*).

Augustine reminds us that these praise songs are more than sweet hymns that have no relation to our lives. That would be mere sentimentality. "Look, you tell me, I am singing. Yes, you are singing. I can hear you. But make sure your life does not contradict your words. Sing with your voices, your hearts, your lips, and your lives. If you desire to praise him, then live what you express. Live good lives and then you yourselves will be his praise" (*Sermon 34*).

In other words, the love of music is not enough. It must be the music of love, of lives really responding to the love we have accepted from God. The hymns we hear in Revelation 19:1-10 are songs rising from Christian witnesses whose lives identified with the Lamb, slain and risen. Each singer is a case study in the Passover mystery, a person whose life was one of Christian struggle, illustrating the discipleship of Jesus who said, "Lose your self, take the cross, follow me." The music of the redeemed is more than an aesthetic experience. It is the outcome of an ascetic life, the way of the cross that leads to a personal Easter because of the power of the victorious Lamb.

In this chapter we hear the final song of the redeemed at the end of the world. Yet we should remember that all over the world in thousands of convents, monasteries, religious houses, mission stations, underground in China, above ground in New York and in cathedrals staffed with canons, these praise songs are heard every day in morning prayer (also called "lauds" which means praises). We also joyfully acknowledge that millions of laity begin their day with praises of God, either at the Eucharist or with the Liturgy of the Hours or with devotional prayers. Redemption is in process right now, not just at the end of time. The grateful response of praise exists right here.

These praise songs nourish our souls with divine beauty and also teach us the way of salvation. St. Ambrose tells us: "In a psalm, instruction vies with beauty. We sing for pleasure. We learn for profit. What experience is not covered by the psalms? I come across the words, 'A song for the beloved,' and I am aflame with desire for God's love. I go through God's revelation in all its beauty, the intimations of resurrection, the gifts of his promise. . . . What is a psalm but a musical instrument to give expression to all the virtues? The psalmist of old used it, with the aid of the Holy Spirit, to make earth re-echo the music of heaven. He used the dead gut of strings to create harmony from a variety of notes, in order to send up to heaven a song of God's praise" (*Commentary on Psalm 1*).

Scripture always connects faith with works, word with example, song with behavior. This first section of chapter 19 concludes with just such a teaching. "Worship God. Witness to Jesus is the spirit of prophecy" (verse 10). Adoring God is an act of faith. Witnessing to Jesus is the application of faith to our daily lives. The verse connects the words "witness" and "prophecy." In Scripture a prophet is a witness to God's word. To be prophetic is to do what God asks of us. God expects us to share our faith both in personal testimony as well as in Christian example in the personal and social order.

The King of Kings and Lord of Lords (19:11-21)

"Then I saw the heavens opened and there was a white horse. Its rider was called 'Faithful and True.'. . . He has a name written on his cloak and on his thigh, 'King of kings and Lord of lords'" (verses 11,16). In chapter 6:2 we saw the first rider on a white horse. He was one of the four horsemen of the Apocalypse, one of those who came to afflict the world with devastation. He is different from the rider we see here. This one is Jesus Christ. He is named the Word of God.

Actually, this triumphant figure is given three names: (1) Faithful and True; (2) Word of God; and, (3) King of kings. To call him Faithful and True means that he both has truth and acts out the truth he tells us. As Word of God he is the Logos — Son of God — who became flesh to save us. As King of kings, he is the conqueror of sin and death.

From Time to Eternity

He comes to bring us from time to eternity, our heavenly goal. History has given us four paths to eternity.

1. *The first is the story of Eden or Paradise.* This causes in us a yearning to go backward in time to the golden age, the good old days, to the garden of delights. But this is retrogression. This is nostalgia. God placed a fiery angel at the gate of Eden and forbade us to go back. We have a similar image in Lot's wife who was told to leave Sodom and not look back. She disobeyed the order and was turned into a pillar of salt. We cannot reverse history. Walking back to an imagined paradise will freeze us and paralyze our souls. We feed on fantasy which causes malnutrition in our souls. This results in the incredibly shrinking heart. The real reason why Eden is not enough is that it is only the beginning of time. We want to get out of time into eternity.

2. *The second path from time to eternity is taught by the eastern religions.* They teach that time is an illusion. Our desires, thoughts, and egos are illusions. We must do all we can to escape time's control of our lives. We should let go of our desires, thoughts, and

egos. The problem with this approach is that we leave this world, but we do not go anywhere.

We empty the glass of its water, but it is never filled with wine. We blank our minds but they do not receive the light of truth. We quiet our desires, but since we want nothing, that is just what we get. The Buddhist word for timelessness is nirvana, which means extinction — not a very promising future. The oriental path does not take us from time to eternity. It just puts us on a wheel where we keep escaping, but arrive nowhere.

3. *Secularism gives us the third path from time to eternity.* The only trouble is that secularists simply promise us heaven on earth, which is merely more time here. They would call it quality time — or utopia. But utopia means nowhere. Marxism promised the dictatorship of the proletariat. We all see what happened to that. Behavioral scientists tell us they can give us a kind of eternity with social engineering and behavioral modification. If we control nature with technology we will be happy.

Of course that has not happened. Where it has been tried, people are unhappier than before. Promises of a kingdom of God on earth are false. Jesus said clearly, "My kingdom does not belong to this world" (Jn. 18:36). Secularism denies eternity so it cannot lead us from time to eternity. It can only give us shallow promises of an ideal state and culture, which will not and cannot happen here.

4. *The Bible gives us the fourth path from time to eternity and this is the real one.* It is the gift from Jesus Christ our Savior. It is his kingdom of God. We already savor its reality here on earth through membership in the Body of Christ, through the food of the sacraments, through the divine love that courses through our souls to one another, and to the world. Grace makes possible the tasting of eternity even in time. It is the pledge of our future glory.

The beauty of the Eden story is not its attracting us to walk backward, but its motivation to rush forward from time to heaven. Heaven is not behind us. It is ahead of us. Jesus, the rider on the white horse, gallops ahead of us to lead us to absolute love and joy. We are born with an inner passion for nothing less than the infinite. Eden is still finite. Eastern religions lock us into the revolving wheel of time, even when showing us how to escape its prison.

Secularism merely deceives us with political and economic candy. It had told us that religion is the opium of the people. Actually, we now know that secularism is the real drug dulling our senses so we fail to see how badly off we are. Christ's religion is the vitamin of the soul. It fills us with energy to race from time to eternity.

This is what the King of kings brings to us. He told us the truth about our human condition and was faithful in showing us how to get out of its problems. He is the Word of God who knew best what would save us. That is why "the armies of heaven followed him, mounted on white horses and wearing white linen" (verse 14).

The Angel Stood on the Sun

The last verses of this chapter (17-21) contain grisly descriptions of what happens to those who trap themselves in their own evil. The cast of characters return — the beasts, the kings, the false prophet (Antichrist). Again they fight against Christ. Again they endure ghastly defeat. Once more they are thrown alive into the fiery pool burning with sulphur. An angel stood on the sun and called the vultures of the air to come and feed on the flesh of the evil ones. "And all the birds gorged themselves on their flesh" (verse 21).

The Wedding of the Lamb

"Blessed are those who have been called to the wedding feast of the Lamb" (verse 9). We should conclude this chapter with the feast that counts most for us. On earth, that is the Passover banquet of the Holy Eucharist. In heaven it will be the spiritual union of love with the Holy Trinity, the Blessed Mother, the angels, and the saints.

The Eucharist is a sacrifice and a meal. It is Good Friday's immolation of the Lamb. It is Easter Sunday's Emmaus Meal. There is no point in killing a lamb and roasting it if no one ever eats it. There is little meaning in Christ's sacrifice if we never commune with his sacred, sacrificed body and blood.

When the Hebrews were in Egypt and suffering under the

oppression of the Pharaoh, God sent an avenging angel to kill all the firstborn. The Jews would be spared if they sacrificed a lamb and marked their door posts with the blood of the lamb. What is often forgotten is that they feasted on the sacrificed lamb. The salvation of their firstborn was not just achieved by an impersonal smearing of blood on their tent poles. They also united themselves to the lamb made sacred by its being offered to God. Personal union with God and obedience to his will was the real key to their liberation.

In Revelation we see the wedding feast of the Lamb, slain and risen, a sacrificed Lamb. The redeemed commune at the table of the Lamb. A sacrifice without communion is like having a cause with no effect. A communion without a sacrifice is similar to an effect with no cause, which makes the experience meaningless. Eucharist is both a sacrifice and a meal. Calvary and Easter are present in mystery by the power of Jesus Christ. By our participation in Eucharist we experience Jesus dying and rising in us. By our Christian witness we undergo the dying and rising of Jesus in our daily lives of pain and joy, of tough giving and exalted receiving. We empty ourselves that others may be full — and so find our hearts more full of love than before.

Our repeated living of the sacrificial and communal aspects of Eucharist are anticipations of heaven. The more we live Eucharist the more we identify with the heavenly wedding banquet. So, when at our deaths we hear the angel say, "Blessed are those who have been called to the wedding feast of the Lamb," we will feel comfortably at home forever.

Reflection

1. What role does music play in my life?
2. In what way do the psalms and hymns of the church affect my faith?
3. What hymns or psalms do I use to praise God?
4. A bell is not a bell till you ring it. A song is not a song till you sing it. How does this apply to my life?
5. The rider on the white horse is faithful and true. Why must fidelity be connected to having the truth?

6. What kind of hope do I derive from the story of Eden in Genesis?
7. What is basically wrong with the paradise promised us by secularism?
8. What does it mean to say I touch eternity in time by my participation in the sacraments?
9. If I say the Eucharist is a meal and not a sacrifice, what do I miss? If I say it is only a sacrifice and not a meal, what is absent? Why do I need both views?
10. Why does Jesus use a wedding banquet as an image for heaven?

Prayer

Magnificent Host of heaven's wedding banquet, feed us now with eternal life. Teach us to identify with your sacrificial love that we may be willing to spend each moment loving others. Awaken us to the gift of love in your sacrificial meal that we may have an abundance of love to offer others. Motivate us to make the Eucharist the center of our lives. It is the banquet on earth that gets us ready for heaven. I praise you, Jesus, most blessed Sacrament of life and love.

20 Millennium — Christ's Thousand-Year Reign

"The Late Great Planet Earth" (20:1-15)

The expression "a thousand years" appears six times in the first seven verses of this chapter. Christians have debated its meaning ever since the days of the early church. Is John describing a future historical event or is he speaking symbolically? One school of interpretation thinks he means a literal reign of Jesus on earth for a thousand years. The other school views his teaching as a symbolic description of the "era of the church" between Christ's first coming in Galilee and his second coming at the end of time. Today, Fundamentalists espouse the literal, historical view. The Catholic Church judges the matter to be symbolic. In this chapter I will compare the Fundamentalist and Catholic approaches to the millennium.

The current, widespread popularity of the Fundamentalist interpretation owes its energy to *The Late Great Planet Earth* by Hal Lindsey and C.C. Carlson, a book that has sold over 15 million copies. The swift approach of the year 2000 provides an urgent interest in millenarianism. Extraordinary political and religious change fuels these millenarian fires all the more. The sudden collapse of the Communist empire in Eastern Europe, the dramatic rise of Islamic Fundamentalism and the controversies surrounding the state of Israel supply millenarians with arguments to support their views.

Contrast this with the "Great Satan" of secularism in Western Europe, North America, and the economic dynamos of the Pacific Rim. Is not the global conflict between the forces of God and Satan clear proof that the millennium is about to appear? That is the question the Fundamentalists raise.

These rapid, worldwide changes give us the context for the discussion of the literal view of Christ's thousand-year reign. Fundamentalists mine these global changes for examples to prove their theories. I should point out immediately that today's millenarians hotly dispute among themselves how this exactly will happen. I will not describe their divergent and complicated opinions. I will simply set out their general scenario for the end of time. Just remember that their basic assumption is that John 20 is a concrete, historical description of the last days.

The Four Last Things

In Catholic thinking, the four last things are: death, judgment, heaven, and hell. In Fundamentalist thinking the four last things are: Rapture, Tribulations, Thousand-Year Reign of Christ, Second Coming. What is meant by each of these steps?

1. *Rapture.* The teaching on Rapture comes from a literal reading of Paul's First Letter to the Thessalonians. "For the Lord himself, with a word of command, with the voice of an archangel and with the trumpet of God, will come down from heaven, and the dead in Christ will rise first. Then we who are alive, who are left, will be caught up together with them in the clouds to meet the Lord in the air. Thus we shall always be with the Lord" (I Thes. 4:16-17).

The idea of rapture derives from the image of the just men and women being "caught up" to meet the Lord "in the air." This Rapture is the first step marking the last days. The just people who rise from the dead will join the faithful people on earth in this ascension into the air to meet Jesus.

Author Jerry Johnston tells us, "Worldwide there is going to be a global evacuation of Christians from the earth at that divine moment. Talk about a news story — the rapture of Christians will rock news bureaus internationally like no other story in human history! . . . Imagine what it will be like on the highways of the world's busiest cities when Christians vanish. Consider the airways . . . pilots, copilots and flight attendants gone! Many business executives, factory workers, mothers, fathers and young people will be gone! . . . The rapture will mean a great reunion."[*]

Catholics interpret this passage from Thessalonians in terms of the Second Coming of Jesus. It is a description of the end of time, not a Rapture preceding a historical thousand-year reign of Jesus.

Catholics remain reserved on how this will happen. The physical image of ascending in the air at the end at best is seen as a symbol of the resurrection of the body. No significant attempt is made to see more in it than that.

It is a mystery of faith, to which texts of the New Testament allude. For example, Paul tells the Corinthians that when the last trumpet sounds, we shall all be changed in the blink of an eye (I Cor. 15:51-52). These allusions and images help us to affirm the truth of the Second Coming and the resurrection of our bodies. Meditations, based on this truth of faith, strengthen our belief, give us hope, but do not necessarily present us with an exact picture of how and when this will occur.

2. *Seven Years of Tribulations.* The Fundamentalists argue that seven years of tribulations will be part of the last days. They base their position on the Last Judgment sermons of Jesus, the predictions of Daniel and Ezekiel, and the extensive lists of woes in Revelation — the ones described by the seven seals, seven trumpets, and seven bowls of wrath. But Fundamentalists differ as to when these will happen. One group says the tribulations will precede the thousand-year reign of Jesus. The other interpreters claim this will occur after the reign and just before the Second Coming.

So the seven years of tribulations are either the second or the third step in their apocalyptic vision, depending on the school of thought. Since most of them see the battle of Armageddon as part of the age of tribulations, the same dispute remains as to when this would happen.

Catholic interpreters agree that tribulations will accompany the

[*]
The Last Days of Planet Earth (Eugene, Ore: Harvest House, 1991), pp. 94, 97.

end of time just as Jesus and John teach. Beyond that, little can be said. Whether the years will be seven or forty-three or ninety-six, no one knows. As to Armageddon, I have already commented on that in chapter 16:16. The best thing is to forget tying these predictions to particular historical dates and concentrate on the spiritual message of any tribulations. Blessed is the one who watches and prays, who is always personally prepared for the coming of the Lord, no matter when it might happen.

　　3. *The Millennium—Christ's Thousand-Year Reign.* Millennium comes from two Latin words — *mille* (meaning thousand) and *annus* (meaning year). Sometimes people call it chiliasm, from the Greek word *chilios* meaning a thousand. Chapter 20 of Revelation is the only place in the Bible where this is explicitly mentioned. Fundamentalists believe it means that Jesus and the saints will rule the world for a thousand years before his Second Coming. The kingdom of God will be realized on earth in a kind of Christian utopia.

　　The Devil will lose his power during this time. Jesus and the martyrs will reign. "I also saw the souls of those who had been beheaded for their witness to Jesus. . . . They came to life and they reigned with Christ for a thousand years" (verse 4). The rest of the dead will not rise until the thousand years are over. When the thousand years are over, Satan will be released to cause the many tribulations that will precede the Second Coming. Then the resurrection of all the dead will occur. The Last Judgment of everyone will happen. All people will be judged according to their deeds. "Anyone whose name was not found written in the book of life was thrown into the pool of fire" (verse 15).

　　Some Christians in the early church, much like modern Fundamentalists, believed in a literal millennium on earth. They were the Christians who had received their training from Jewish converts to the church. Some strains of Jewish tradition at that time foresaw a millennium on earth in which the messiah would establish his kingdom. Rabbis argued whether this would be 1,000, 2,000, or 7,000 years. Though they emphasized this would be a kingdom of justice and peace, they described it in terms of physical blessings of abundant forests, vines, wine, no hostility between people and beasts, no pain in childbirth, and so on.

Millenarianism was never a universal teaching of the early church, but it did win supporters here and there. Distinguished teachers such as Justin Martyr and Tertullian believed in it. The break with that tradition came with Origen who presented a symbolic understanding of Scripture. The saints will eat, but it will be the bread of life. They will drink, but from the cup of wisdom.

Augustine completed what Origen started. The thousand years means the "era of the church," the time between Christ's birth at Bethlehem and his Second Coming. The rule of the saints is the victory of the kingdom of Christ in human hearts that surrender to him in faith. The judgment given to the saints is the power of the Sacrament of Reconciliation in which sins are bound and sinners released to freedom and forgiveness. The first resurrection described in chapter 20 is the welcoming into heaven of the saints who die before the Second Coming. Augustine spiritualized the whole teaching of chapter 20 and that is how the Catholic Church has accepted it ever since.

4. *The Second Coming.* Recall where we have been up to this point in our overview of the four last things taught by Fundamentalists: (1) Rapture; (2) Tribulations; (3) Millennium.

The fourth step is the Second Coming of Jesus and the Last Judgment. For them this only happens after the Rapture, the Tribulations, and the Millennium. The Second Coming of Jesus Christ will involve the Last Judgment of the living and the dead, the sending of the unrepentant sinners to hell and the welcoming of the just to heaven.

Because they follow the literal interpretation of these texts, Fundamentalists try to nail down a date for the Second Coming. Despite repeated failures of numerous earlier predictions of the world's end, they continue to believe they can figure it out. Each failure is followed by a reconsideration of some factor ignored in the previous prediction, thus allowing a new scenario to be proposed. This seems to be a useless passion.

Catholics affirm their faith in the Second Coming with the words in the Nicene Creed, "He will come again in glory to judge the living and the dead." Though Catholics do not speak of the rapture, they do subscribe to a glorious, final manifestation of Christ at the end of time. The Catholic view of the millennium is that Christ's kingdom of love, justice, peace, and salvation has already become available to believers through grace, faith, active membership in the church, active participation in the sacraments, and a Christian moral life.

The Spiritual Power of Christ's Second Coming

Most discussions about Christ's Second Coming concentrate so much on timing or on the cosmic fireworks that will accompany it, that the spiritual value of the teaching is lost. Christ's promise to come again speaks to a human need that is always endangered by the daily troubles, trials, and tragedies that depress us. Life's indignities can so overwhelm us that we tend to lose hope. The proverb says that hope springs eternal in the human heart, but in fact a great deal of hopelessness afflicts all too many people.

Our practical natures rightly look for concrete solutions to the vacuum of hope. Support groups, networks of helping professionals, hot lines, social programs, government initiatives, and many similar valuable forms of outreach try to stem the tide of losing hope. We should continue these forms of caring and intensify their availability and effectiveness.

At the same time we should realize that practical responses are but one of two essential ways to reply to hopelessness. The other is the spiritual response. I began this book by asking the question, "Does God really care about us?" I pointed out that this is the question embedded in Revelation and that the answer is yes. Practical caring for people, without a spiritual counterpart, runs the risk of treating a symptom and ignoring the cause. The role of the spiritual is to address the cause of hope's decline. This is not an either-or matter. We need both the practical and the spiritual responses.

God has planted deep within our hearts a desire for perfect happiness and the hope that it can be found. We are born as lovers who expect our beloved will come. Pain, disappointment, death, disease, war, loss, betrayal, injury, and hatred seem to cheat us of our hope. First they distract us. Then they erode our confidence. Finally they tempt us to despair. Our beloved will not come after all.

The doctrine of the final coming of Jesus Christ is meant to sustain the fire of our hope-filled expectation. No matter how terrible be the ills we face in life, we can be certain that our beloved will come to fulfill our most fundamental hope. We might object that we do not think we will be around for the actual Second Coming. We will most likely die before that great day. What good is a Second Coming that we will probably never experience here? How can we keep moving on life's journey, with its sea of troubles, when we will probably not meet the beloved who says he is coming? The answer is that Christ's Second Coming at the end of time has already begun. Human time does not restrict Jesus. A thousand years are like a moment in his perspective. Jesus is already here in our midst. What his Second Coming will accomplish is the public display of his glory at the end of history. But we can already experience his presence right now. The Second Coming at the end of history will be a visible appearance of Jesus. His Second Coming in our own personal lives is invisible. St. Bernard tells us, "This coming is a hidden one. In it, only the elect see the Lord within themselves." The process is this: Our hearts hope for absolute and perfect fulfillment. We expect our beloved to come to us. Jesus tells us that he will come right now as well as at the end. "I am with you all days, even to the end of the world" (cf. Mt. 28:20).

The public Second Coming of Jesus will be accompanied by his last judgment on all peoples. St. Matthew records Christ's description of this in terms of Christian behavior. Those who fed, clothed, and cared for others will be saved, because they did it to Christ himself. Those who failed to do this will be damned.

What then should be our belief, attitude, and behavior between the times? First we should reaffirm our faith that Jesus, our beloved, is already coming into our lives to satisfy our deepest longings. Secondly, we should have an attitude infused with hope despite all signals that would rob us of it. The attitude gives us the aptitude for love.

Thirdly, we should engage in constant acts of love and concern. Each act of love deepens our hope. Each time we reach out with care and concern for others causes a surge of hope to arise in our hearts. Love is the key to hope. Why? Because we not only love the person we see, but also the Christ we do not see. We display a confidence that our beloved is in fact right here. We love others because of

Jesus. We love Jesus because of others who give us such a splendid opportunity to pour out ourselves for them — and him. Every person we meet is a sign of grace, a symbol of the coming of Jesus.

Such is the immense spiritual value of the doctrine of the Second Coming. Our hourly prayer should be, "Come, Lord Jesus!" Be assured that his answer always is: "Have hope. I am here!"

Reflection

1. If someone asked me what I think of the end of the world, what would I say?
2. What is the basic difference between the Catholic view of the end of time and that of Fundamentalists?
3. What is happening in our world today that might make me think the end of time is about to happen?
4. If a Fundamentalist tried to convince me about the Rapture as the beginning of the millennium, how would I respond?
5. Why is it best that I see the millennium as the "era of the church" and not a literal thousand-year reign of Jesus on earth?
6. Why did some early Catholic teachers believe in a literal millennium?
7. What experiences of encounters with hopelessness have I had that I could share with others?
8. How do I help others who are depressed and losing hope?
9. How will I apply the doctrine of the Second Coming in my personal life?
10. What victories of hope over despair have I known in my life?

Prayer

Lord Jesus, you are my gift of hope. Your Second Coming has already begun in my life because your glory-presence has been manifested to me. Your drive of love toward me responds to my inmost push of love toward you. Because of this my sense of hope is always nourished and in a growth pattern. I find that every act of love for others enhances my hope. I praise you for the gift of your presence and your constant coming into my life.

21 The New Jerusalem — My Happy Home

Who Can Be Happy in Heaven? (21:1-8)

Am I convinced that heaven will make me perfectly happy?
It all depends.

Scripture says that holiness is the absolute qualification for entering heaven. God calls us to be forgiving, pure of heart, humble, loving, self-denying, responsible, honest, true, generous, and chaste if we hope to enjoy heaven. Faith in Jesus and obedience to his will are necessary for entering his kingdom. Yet we find ourselves weak, sinful, and prone to moral apathy rather than sturdily pursuing a life of virtue. We are much better at breaking the ten commandments than keeping them. While we praise the Sermon on the Mount, we are more likely to live by the sermons of the secular culture.

Since that is how we usually find ourselves, would it not be better if God would somehow save us without our becoming virtuous?

Why do we have to be holy in order to enjoy heaven? First of all, what is holiness? It is living by the power of the Holy Spirit. Holiness calls us to refuse to live by the destructive ideals of the secular culture, to resist the temptations of Satan/Father of Lies, to overcome the leaden seductions of the "flesh," — aggressive self-centeredness. Holiness summons us to discover God's commandments as methods for loving self, others, and God. Holiness asks us to obey God's will and to nurture an affection for the world to come, so that we already begin to feel at home there in the midst of this life.

The biggest mistake we make about heaven is that we think it is like earth. Our view of earth is a place where we choose what will make us happy. We see people looking for happiness in all kinds of ways. Politicians, farmers, business-people, writers, scientists, authors, computer-hackers, priests, bishops, nuns, monks, sailors, soldiers, dancers, actors have their own pursuits and pleasures. We assume the next world will be very much the same. We imagine the unique difference between earth and heaven is that we will be certain that what we seek will be found. Here we always have some doubt and sense of risk. There, we will be confident that our search works.

We do acknowledge that we should be reconciled to God's will. But we treat that as a side issue. We will get around to it just in time before we die. At best we use our average attention to religious requirements as a sort of nuisance factor to which we give a swift nod and get on with the business of earthly pursuits. We lose sleep over finding happiness in passing matters here. We do our sleeping when dealing with divine issues, not just at boring sermons, but in our own inner life when called to come to terms with God.

Heaven Is Not Like Earth

Scripture clearly teaches that heaven is not a place where people find their pleasure in pursuing their personal interests. The discordant and competing roads to pleasure on earth will not happen in heaven. Our happiness will be doing what pleases God. Chapter 21 of Revelation makes it clear that heaven is much different from earth. Heaven will be a "city that had no need of the sun or moon to shine on it, for the glory of God gave it light, and its lamp was the Lamb" (verse 23).

John insists that heaven is radically different. "I saw a new heaven and a new earth" (verse 1). In this new experience "God's dwelling is with the human race. He will dwell with them and they will be his people and God himself will always be with them. He will wipe every tear away from their eyes, and there shall be no more death or mourning, wailing or pain, for the old order has passed away" (verses 3, 4).

In John's view, heaven is an environment that is resolutely God-centered. "I am the Alpha and the Omega, the beginning and the end" (verse 6). Earth is a place that is occasionally God-centered in some people's lives, and then only with a struggle. If the truth be told, earth is a world that is human-centered. Now God is human-centered too. Why else did the Son of God become a human being? What then is the difference? People are so human-centered they see nothing beyond the human. God is human-centered for the purpose of fulfilling humanity, of making achievable the deepest drive for the infinite in every person. Earth has a smiling face. That is why we love it so much. That is why we expect heaven to be more of the same.

But earth is not like heaven. John writes of an earth that supports self-destructive behavior. "But as for cowards, the unfaithful, the depraved, murderers, the unchaste, sorcerers, idol-worshipers, and deceivers of every sort, their lot is in the burning pool of fire and sulphur, which is the second death" (verse 8). On the other hand, the considerable pleasures of heaven occur because we will always be doing God's will.

Jerusalem, My Happy Home (21:9-27)

Cardinal Newman compares heaven to a church. "Heaven is like a church. For in a place of public worship no language of this world is heard. There are no schemes brought forward for temporal objects, great or small. No information on how to strengthen our worldly interests, extend our influence or establish our credit. These things may indeed be right in their way, so that we do not set our hearts upon them. Still, it is certain we hear nothing of them in a church. Here we hear solely and entirely of God. We praise him, worship him, sing to him, thank him, confess to him, give ourselves up to him, and ask his blessing. Therefore, a church is like heaven, because both in the one and the other, there is one, single sovereign subject — religion — brought before us."[*]

This corresponds perfectly with John's word pictures of heaven in Revelation. I already alluded to this when meditating with you on the liturgical quality of his descriptions of heaven. He drew from the hymns, rituals, prayers, and mood of adoration of God that he

---

[*] *Parochial and Plain Sermons*, (San Francisco: Ignatius Press, 1987), p. 7.

presided over in the house liturgies of his own time to tell us what heaven will be like. I should repeat here that we are dealing with mystery. I echo again Paul's caution about describing heaven too literally. No eye has seen, nor ear heard what God has prepared for us. When John or Cardinal Newman use the comparison of a church or a liturgical ceremony, they do not ask us to dwell on the ceremonies or the music, but on the essential message which is a God-centered experience.

Focusing on God alone and doing his will may not seem like a recipe for perfect happiness. Yet God says, "To the thirsty I will give a gift from the spring of life-giving water" (verse 6). God will wash away all tears, remove all mourning, wailing, pain, and death. Are these not signs of the possibilities of happiness? God will fulfill us far more adequately than any self-help technique offered us today. No matter how much we fulfill ourselves with numerous — and admittedly useful techniques — we still cry, we continue to feel depressed, we often get sick, we always die and leave someone to mourn our passing.

Why Can't an Unrepentant Sinner Enjoy Heaven?

Look at it this way. Do you think an anti-religious person could derive continuous and lasting joy from participating in Eucharist? Can militant secularists really find meaning for their lives in worshiping God? Would hostile unbelievers be thrilled by messages about something they do not care about? Could they be charmed by a Gospel challenge that for them does not excite them and engage their hopes and energies? How then could these people enjoy heaven?

If sinners are not happy with God on earth, can they expect happiness with him in heaven? Would not unbelievers and sinners be terribly disappointed by heaven? They would find no communication that delighted them on earth. They would not come upon the activities which gave them pleasure on earth. They would be terribly lonely. On earth they had put a wall around their hearts that kept God out. They did that freely and would arrive in heaven with the wall intact. Only now there would be no place to go.

The lights of the earthly city have gone out — passed away. The clubs are closed. The drugs are gone. The sex has vanished. The whiskey bottles are empty. The whips and guns used to degrade and dehumanize others no longer exist. Banks have crumbled and gold has returned to dust. Diamonds are not forever. There is no more need for scientific discoveries, new novels to write, new pictures to paint, new clothes to wear.

Worse yet they could not bear to look on the face of God whom on earth they considered to be the source of human unhappiness. God's love would give them no pleasure in heaven because on earth they had convinced themselves that it was irrelevant. They feel alone. As they sense the face they rejected they are like the demons that looked at Jesus and they repeat the cry, "Leave us alone! We have nothing to do with you!" The unholy cannot bear to look at God. They did not want to do it on earth. They cannot do it in heaven. No, sinners cannot enjoy heaven. They choose a different and illusory way to be happy. It is a tragic option. It is not all that satisfactory for them on earth anyhow. In heaven it would be an impossibility.

The Twelve Gates of the City

John takes a poetic memory of the glory of the earthly Jerusalem to portray heaven. His emphasis is on the glory of God. If he uses images of jewels and ivory, it is not to focus on earthly treasures but to make us think of God's beauty. The new Jerusalem "gleamed with the splendor of God" (verse 11). John expands on God's beauty by imagining the Lord and city decorated with twelve jewels: jasper, sapphire, chalcedony, emerald, sardonyx, carnelian, chrysolite, beryl, topaz, chrysoprase, hyacinth, and amethyst.

The pictures of the glittering jewels captivate our imaginations in order to get our attention. We must let the images speak to our hearts where God dwells waiting to tell us he is infinitely greater than any of that. Do not be distracted by the physical splendor. John's true focus is on the grandeur and splendor of the transcendent God.

The twelve gates to the city of God consist of one vast pearl, the most valued of precious stones. The use of twelve in this chapter is based on the twelve apostles. "The wall of the city had twelve courses of stones as its foundation, on which were inscribed the twelve names of the twelve apostles of the Lamb" (verse 14).

It seems like an earthly paradise, but it is not. "There will be no night there" (verse 25). Ancient peoples, like children today, were afraid of the dark. In heaven there will be no scary night for God is pure light. His presence is like the comforting warmth of the sun. He will be the perfect satisfaction of our mind's quest for truth and the absolute fulfillment of our hearts need for the warmth of love.

Get Ready for Heaven

If heaven's joy is caused by doing what God wants with selfless love, then preparing for heaven demands acting that way on earth. What does God want? God commands us to love him, others, and self. This is spelled out in the ten commandments and Christ's commentary on them in the Sermon on the Mount (Matthew 5-7). Thousands of verses of Scripture carry commands that show us how to love. The sheer variety of these biblical urgings may confuse us unless we simplify the whole matter as Jesus himself did when he gave us the laws of love. He repeats them when he reminds us that the only way we know we love him is when we keep his commandments.

Love is the royal road to heaven. Life in heaven is a rapturous communion of love. It is ecstasy in the truest and final sense. Ecstasy comes from a Greek word that means being outside oneself. Every act of love on earth, from the smallest to the greatest, is a form of ecstasy, a way of getting out from under the spell of the control of our "selves." We tend not to notice the small ecstasies but occasionally are overwhelmed by a profound religious experience of God when his grace has caused us to perform a great act of love.

We should distinguish great deeds from great love. Mother Teresa says that it is not important to perform great deeds, just to do little ones with great love. Most days of our lives are passed in doing ordinary things. Virtually all of us are ordinary people. And even the so-called powerful and famous people of the world must engage in a large number of simple and prosaic acts each day. The diaries and biographies of famous people testify to this.

The most ordinary of persons is capable of the greatest love. The simplest acts of the humblest human can bear the weight of glory when done with love. A billionaire may hug a child in a hurried and perfunctory way. A welfare mother may hug her baby with rapturous affection. Money and fame do not assure love's abundance. Of course neither does poverty. A person on a low income could treat another with scorn, while a king is perfectly capable of treating another with a touching innocence and heart-swelling love. It all depends on what a given person wants to do. The option for love is the most democratic of all choices, available to everyone on the planet earth.

The practice of love is a dress rehearsal for heaven. Loving God, others, and self is a training exercise for heaven. The Holy Spirit is available to make this love happen to those who have faith and hope. The life of love on earth prepares us for heaven. If we do not enjoy loving here, we will fail to like heaven because God is love and we will feel out of place there. If I dislike baseball, I am not going to enjoy it by going to a ball park. If I cannot stand classical music, I am not likely to suddenly enjoy it in a concert hall. Preparation and conversion are necessary.

God's creation speaks to us of his love and the heaven where love thrives. The Book of Revelation tells us that this world will be replaced with a new heaven and a new earth. There will be a transformation. Cardinal Newman describes this transfiguration:

All that we see is destined one day to burst forth into a heavenly bloom, and to be transfigured into immortal glory. The sun will grow pale and be lost in the sky, but it will be before the radiance of him whom it does but image, the Sun of Righteousness.
He will come forth as a bridegroom out of his chamber. The stars will be replaced by saints and angels surrounding his throne. Above and below, the clouds of the air, the trees of the field and the waters of the great deep will be impregnated with the forms of everlasting spirits, the servants of God which do his pleasure. And our own mortal bodies will be found to contain within them the inner person, which will then receive its due proportion as the soul's harmonious organ. For this glorious manifestation the whole creation is at present in travail, earnestly desiring that it may be accomplished in its season.[*]

---

[*] *Op. Cit.*, p. 867.

We all know that fire transforms into itself what it touches. Physical fire is the image of human love. Just as fire changes what it affects, so love transforms those its touches. Even if love fails to change one or another person, it always transforms the lover. Every time I truly love, I am changed into love. Remember that authentic love removes us away from self-centeredness. We lose the selfish self and gain the loving "I." Eventually, even the "I" focuses on the "not-I" which is God. Love has brought us to the first glimmerings of heaven even here on earth.

Our faith tells us that the grace for this is found in the food of the sacraments, especially the Eucharist. Jesus is love. Our union with him transforms us into living acts of love and persons alive with affection. Thus we carry heaven already here. Hence we will feel right at home when we get to heaven. The only question we will have is, "Why did we have to wait so long to get there?"

Reflection

1. How often do I think of heaven? When I do think of heaven what comes to my mind?
2. Holiness is a condition for enjoying heaven. What words would I use to describe holiness?
3. We use earthly images to describe heaven, but heaven is not like earth. Why not?
4. Why can't unrepentant sinners enjoy heaven?
5. Cardinal Newman compares heaven to a church. What is he trying to say?
6. Some say God should save us in spite of our commitment to sin. Why is that an unworkable idea?
7. What is John trying to teach when he uses twelve jewels to describe heaven?
8. Why is love on earth the best preparation for heaven?
9. Love, like fire, transforms. But if my love does not change another, how is love transforming?
10. What can I do to increase my awareness of heaven and prepare to go there?

Prayer

Jesus, purest love, you came to earth to help me get to heaven. You honored my humanity that I may be divinized by your Holy Spirit. You planted in my human life a hunger for divine life and then provided me with the means to achieve it. Remind me that even on earth I can begin to experience heaven through every act of love of God, others and self. Open my heart to the Eucharist, the most heavenly of sacraments, that I may experience your transformation.

22 Come, Lord Jesus! Yes, I Am Coming Soon!

When Pope John XXIII was asked about the next life, he said, "My bags are packed. I am ready to go."

In the Old Testament, David said, "Even though I walk in the dark valley, I fear no evil, for you are at my side" (Ps. 23:4). In the New Testament, Paul said, "If I go on living in the flesh, that means fruitful labor for me. And I do not know which I shall choose. I am caught between the two. I long to depart from this life and be with Christ. . . . Yet, that I remain in the flesh is more necessary for your benefit" (Phil. 1:22-24).

David was willing to go but wanted to stay. Paul was willing to stay but wanted to go. There is a bit of David and Paul in all of us. We like the idea of heaven. We feel secure in what we know on earth. Faith pushes us to heaven. Familiarity ties us to earth.

Seventy-seven percent of Americans believe in the existence of heaven. Three out of four Americans believe they have an excellent chance of getting there. Yet Jesus gives us a sobering thought. "How narrow the gate and constricted the road that leads to life. And those who find it are few" (Mt. 7:14). Still we know that God's love reaches out to every person on earth and yearns to bring all to heaven. Facile optimism about getting to heaven is not enough. We have moral responsibilities to fulfill. At the same time gloomy pessimism does not help. There is little point in looking at percentages. Look rather at the preciousness of each man and woman and be filled with the faith, hope, and love that will bring all our brothers and sisters to heaven.

Let All Who Thirst Come to the Waters (22:1-5)

In this final chapter of Revelation, John brings us back to heaven and summarizes the major themes of this book. This time he pictures heaven as a river bursting with God's love and life. "Then the angel showed me the river of life-giving water, sparkling like crystal, flowing from the throne of God and of the Lamb" (verse 1). The tree of life grows by the bank of this river.

This tree appeared in the first book of the Bible in the earthly paradise (Gn. 2:9). It shows up again in the last book of the Bible in the heavenly paradise. The image demonstrates that God stands for life. The human desire for life, to live it more fully, is a gift of God. Jesus the Lamb is the real fullness of life for all of us. If we expect to be really alive both here and hereafter, we must come to Christ, symbolized by the tree of life by the river of divine vitality.

John calls the tree of life a medicine for all nations. If the tree is the medicine, what is the disease? The malady is human sinfulness which leads to pain and death. Jesus offers the healing medicine of mercy. When we allow ourselves to be healed by Christ's loving medicine, we begin to look on the face of God which is a face of love. That means that our heavenly future begins already here on earth and that when we go to heaven we shall be supremely happy in beholding the divine face that shows us nothing but care and affection.

In baptism we figuratively waded into the divine river of life. Through the ministry of the priest who made the sign of the cross on our foreheads, we already anticipate what shall be the sign of our being possessed by God in heaven. The redeemed will "look upon his face, and his name will be on their foreheads" (verse 4).

Poets associate night with death. Children instinctively know this by their fear of the dark and their pleas for a night light and a teddy bear or doll to hug. Jesus often spoke of night as a symbol of sin and death. In heaven the night will disappear because death and sin will not exist there. God, who is perfect light, will replace the sun for us. "Night will be no more, nor will they need light from lamp or sun, for the Lord God shall give them light" (verse 5).

This Revelation Is True (22:6-15)

An angel assures John that all he has seen and heard is really the truth. We should recall that we are dealing with divine truth which is apprehended by faith. We operate on two levels, the human and the divine. Our reason comprehends the truths of this life. Our faith grasps the truths of the life of the Spirit. However, even though we use two different faculties to get at truth, there is a unity between the truths we know. God's truth and the truths of everyday life are all true. There is no contradiction between what is true on earth and what is true in heaven.

One way to appreciate this is to think of love. When we experience real love from another human being, we know it is true love. Similarly, when we feel God's love for us, we know it is true. Love is love, whether human or divine, for God is the author and source of all love. That is why we sing, "Where charity and love prevail, there God is ever found." It is the reason why Paul tells us that love alone of all the virtues will survive in heaven. "Love never fails. . . . When the perfect comes, the partial will pass away. . . . So faith, hope, love remain, but the greatest of these is love" (I Cor. 13:8, 10, 13).

So the angel tells John that the words of Revelation are real truths. Our fact-oriented and rational-minded culture make us think the words of Revelation are wild dreams, peculiar images, so symbolic that they could hardly stand for down-to-earth truth. But the modern world sees life with only one eye, the rational one. We have two eyes in the mind. One perceives with reason and the other with faith. The faith eye, in its human form, is accustomed to poetry, imagery, symbol, and pictures. Why? Because we need human comparisons to sense the action of God in our lives. Theologians call this the principle of analogy — or comparison. We compare the divine truths we believe to pictures which are familiar to us. Why else did Jesus use parables or picture stories to help us grasp divine truths?

The text combines this assurance about truth with a reference to the prophets whom God inspired. This book is a prophetic book that gave meaning to the Christians of John's time in the midst of their sufferings. It also foretells that we would have our own tests of faith in our contemporary world. Lastly, it predicts the truth of the end of this finite world, the judgment on sinners, and the triumphant second coming of Jesus. "Behold, I am coming soon" (verse 7). Jesus comes "soon" in all ages of human history. He does not abandon the faith community at any time in the history of salvation, be that during the ancient Roman persecutions or in this century's communist persecution of millions of believers.

John then gives his own testimony about the truth of his book. "It is I, John, who heard and saw these things" (verse 8). People expect believers to witness personally the truth of what they say. John tells us that he is doing more than teaching a lesson from a book. He is revealing to us the content of his religious experience of God. He does more than share abstract ideas. He discloses something that really happened to him.

The angel warns John not to seal up this prophetic book. Visionaries are often given "secrets" from God, not to be made known until the proper time. In our own day, the famous "Fatima Secret" given to Sister Lucy is just such an example. That secret has been shared only with popes but never made known to the public. We have no idea why it is still concealed after more than seventy-five years. But John must not keep secret or seal up the prophetic book he has written. It contains a message of mercy and consolation for the persecuted church whenever it appears in Christian history.

As history unfolds, the wicked will still act wickedly and the "filthy still be filthy" (verse 11). That should not matter to believers. The outrageous sinfulness of the world should motivate the believers to be more energetic in doing what is right and seeking to be holy. No matter how bad the world may seem, the good people should strive to be better. This must not be a "holier than thou" attitude. Believers should reach out in loving compassion and prayer to unrepentant sinners. After all, believers are forgiven sinners and have their own moral struggles to fight until death.

Jesus comes "soon" at each moment of salvation history and judges people according to their deeds. Time does not restrict him. He is the "Alpha and the Omega, the first and the last, the beginning and the end" (verse 13). The ticking of the clock is not a slow process for him, for he is present to every minute of history. Just as all time is as present to him as this moment is to us, so he stands right next to our heartbeats and lovingly invites us to rest in him, to breathe with love, to accept grace flowing from him.

The next verse praises the believers who have washed their robes clean. The image is drawn from early baptismal ceremonies. The candidates would take off their "old" robe, descend into the baptismal pool to be cleansed by the Holy Spirit of all sin. When they ascended from the pool, they were clothed in a new, white baptismal robe that symbolized their new lives in Christ.

The first readers of this book would know exactly what John is talking about. In the fourth century, the baptismal buildings, usually eight-sided structures, known as baptistries, would have paintings on the walls with the Tree of Life and the River Flowing from the Throne and the Heavenly City With Twelve Gates. Artists borrowed from Revelation for these baptismal themes. The saved have "the right to the tree of life and enter the city through its gates" (verse 14).

The next verse describes those who are barred from God's city. The list includes sorcerers, the unchaste, murderers, idol worshipers, and liars. It also mentions "dogs." That definitely seems strange to us for whom dogs are pets, lovable, our best friends. But in biblical culture dogs were scavengers. They were dirty because they ate garbage. They were considered lazy and they made too much noise at night with their street barking.

Wild packs of dogs were common and their ferocity feared. They licked the sores of the poor man Lazarus, not out of sympathy, but because he was too weak to ward them off. However, dogs in other cultures (Mesopotamian, Greek, and Egyptian) were more favored. Odd as it is to us, dogs in Scripture have a negative reputation. So we find dogs symbolizing sinners barred from the heavenly city.

Come, Lord Jesus! (22:16-21)

In these final verses John is neatly tying together all the great themes of his book. You may recall that he began his message with letters to the seven house churches. He praised their virtues and challenged them to overcome their sins. He gave them a vision of hope in Christ to sustain them through hard times. The Risen Jesus stands at the center of John's message. "I, Jesus, sent my angel to give you (John) this testimony for the churches" (verse 16).

This Jesus is the very root and offspring of David. "But a shoot shall sprout from the stump of Jesse" (Is. 11:1). Jesse was the father of David, who became Israel's most beloved saint — a poet, a warrior, a lover, a sinner, a king, and the embodiment of the nation's soul. When the prophets envisioned the future messiah, they saw him as both a biological descendant of David as well as a spiritual heir to the role David played in the national consciousness. As Son of Mary and foster-son of Joseph, Jesus was born of the house and family of David. As Son of God, Jesus is the "root" of the origin of David.

In the closing lines of the Bible, Jesus reveals himself as the "morning star." It is common enough today to speak of superstars to refer to heroes in sports, entertainment, business, politics and even in the church. We have all heard (or heard of) the rock opera, "Jesus Christ Superstar." The use of a star to illustrate human accomplishment is quite biblical. "A star shall advance from Jacob" (Nm. 24:17). In biblical genealogy, the patriarch Jacob was one of the ancestors of Jesus.

A star fits Jesus so well, for it lifts our eyes beyond the cares of earth, it focuses us on the darkness from which light comes. Sailors look at a star to guide their journey. The magi followed a star to find the infant Jesus. Jesus is more than a celebrity star, he is a sure guide in the midst of our confusion, darkness, and frustration. Better yet, he is a "morning star" assuring us that a new day is beginning.

One of the greatest themes of the New Testament is the invitation to mission. Jesus appointed his apostles and their associates to be missionaries of the Gospel. Salvation must not be hoarded as a private treasure. Love which is stingy becomes selfishness. Salvation which is protected in a hot house ceases to nourish the person who simply lapses into sentimental, self-serving piety. Only when we share Jesus and his love do we flourish with large hearts and the church begins to grow. This is the meaning of the words, "The Spirit and the bride say, 'Come' " (verse 17). The risen Jesus calls the whole world to experience his love, forgiveness, justice, and mercy. He does this through his Spirit and the "bride" which is his church.

What Jesus says, we must say. "Let the hearer say, 'Come.' Let the one who thirsts come forward, and the one who wants it receive the gift of life-giving water" (verse 17). We are the hearers of the Word. Our vocation is to repeat the Word's invitation to salvation to all people. In sharing our faith with others, we speak to those in whom God has planted the thirst for absolute and unfailing love. We open our arms with hospitality to the thirsting ones and welcome those who want it to the life-giving waters of baptism and the life affirming community of the church.

Songs of Joy

On a pilgrimage to Jerusalem, I had the good fortune to be able to celebrate the mysteries of the passion and resurrection during Holy Week. I attended the Easter Vigil at the convent of the Daughters of Zion. Their convent is built where tradition says Pilate's Fortress Antonia stood. I saw the Lithostrotos, the stone pavement upon which Jesus would have stood when he was on trial before Pilate. With that vivid memory of the passion, I joined the other worshipers in the exultant liturgy of the resurrection.

After the liturgy, at about two o'clock in the morning, I took a solitary walk through the streets of the old city of Jerusalem. It was a perfect night. The stars shone with crystal light. I allowed my mind to wander back two thousand years to the days when the first Eucharists were being celebrated. Possibly, many of those involved in the breaking of the bread those first few years after the resurrection were privileged to do so in the very upper room where that blessed event originally occurred. Others would be doing the same in their own upper rooms of their house churches.

I let my imagination collapse time between them and me. About this hour they would have finished their liturgies as I had just done. Their last song would be loud shouts of joy from their rooftops where they gazed at the morning star.

I heard them sing, "Come, Lord Jesus!"

I heard Jesus sing back, "Yes, I am coming soon!"

"Blessed are you and praiseworthy and glorious forever, my Lord Jesus. You sit upon your throne in your kingdom of heaven, in the glory of your divinity, living in the most holy body you took from a virgin's flesh. So you will appear on that last day to judge the souls of all the living and the dead. Unending honor be to you, my Lord Jesus Christ!"

— A Prayer of St. Bridget of Sweden

Reflection

1. How prepared am I for heaven?
2. Three-fourths of Americans believe they have a good chance of getting to heaven. What is the source of their optimism?
3. With all the talk of abortion and doctor-assisted suicide, how will I keep my focus on the value of life and human dignity?
4. How does awareness of my death affect my spiritual and moral behavior?
5. What helps me see the unity between the truths I acquire from reason and those I arrive at in faith?
6. Why is it important that I witness truth as a lived reality?
7. Jesus comes "soon" to me, meaning every second of my life. What steps will assist me to be aware of this?
8. What am I doing to make Jesus the center of my life?
9. What are the various ways I share my faith with others?
10. How does the prayer, "Come, Lord Jesus!" express my own yearning for life, love and God?

Prayer

Worthy are you, Lord Jesus Christ, to receive glory and honor and power. You are the victorious Lamb, slain and risen from the dead. You have made of us a kingdom of love, justice, and mercy. You have formed us into a priestly people, a communion of loving people who offer you a sacrifice of praise. "To the one who sits on the throne and to the Lamb be blessing and honor, glory and might, forever and ever. Amen!" (Rev. 5:13).